MUTABILITY

ANDREA BRADY

**MUTABILITY**
*Scripts for Infancy*

LONDON NEW YORK CALCUTTA

**Seagull Books, 2012**

© Andrea Brady, 2012

ISBN-13      978 0 8574 2 090 9

**British Library Cataloguing-in-Publication Data**
A catalogue record for this book is available from the British Library

Typeset in Arno Pro by Seagull Books, Calcutta, India
Printed and bound by Hyam Enterprises, Calcutta, India

# CONTENTS

## ACKNOWLEDGEMENTS

Excerpts from this text were presented as 'Animate Work', at the Contempo Seminar Series, University of Aberystwyth, on 30 March 2009. My thanks to Peter Barry and Ian Davidson for the invitation, and to everyone who participated in the discussion.

I also want to think some of those with whom I experienced infancy: Jeanette Baartman, Emily Butterworth, Aline Ferrari, Nancy Prior, Hannah Westley, and most especially, Matt ffytche.

all that moueth, doth mutation loue

**1**

To begin with an incident outside
language, beyond recollection,
enforces the solidarity of our work
to build up into sound. Pethedine concussions
and a nozzle of oxygen to plead across
running like a horse, spare us
the knowledge that there is no knowledge
come rushing down, feral.
Effacing into perfect silence,
the working tongue in a yellow corridor.


You are two weeks old. Your face is lacy and you've got small,
light scratches from those questing, autonomous hands: the
first harm inflicted yourself. In the night you warn me with
magpie chutters, the coughs of thirst half-waking, and I tuck
you still waxen under my arm, the milk overspilling at any
approach. You lick it back if I curl alongside you, my whole
body a feeding organism for you. Is it narcissistic to take note
of that? Even if there's no border between us, our wills flut-
tering to match?

Your dark eyes fix the borders of light and shadow, mesmer-
ized in a sticky fixation on contrasts, the first resolution you'll
learn to make. It isn't devotion, fascination or dependency
but a kind of regard which honours, the curve of chin into
hair, seams. Generally you don't complain, even when we lift
you from the bath, whitening your hands when you shake
with primitive tremors: to make anything worse for you is
only forgivable if we can wrap you up in adult fortitude after,
singing to warm you.

*Monday, 21 July 2008*


The roundness of your head exaggerates. Your cheeks plump
with milk strain fine spidery lines of red from all your vigour,
sucking your life out of me. Come to the breast, at one week
old, you are ravished by excitement: a zone of pleasure you

recognize, bob your head round, lick and tease it, hold briefly in your mouth before disengaging, mastering the delight of contact through repetition. You cough and wheeze at its proximity. Some milk cuffed your folded arm, and you went for it, sucking your self as a new site of plenty.

Rousseau describes the child as 'tout entier à son être actuel, et jouissant d'une plenitude de vie qui semble vouloir s'éntendre hors de lui'. I envy your experience of plenitude as repetition, as I give it to you in anticipation of words. Poems as sacks of choices, limits payable for their endless renewal. Their pleasure is a condition of their repeated vacancy: empty them, you find the bottomless refill, always temporarily satisfying the avarice which will reappear, like a ghost on a mechanical platform. So the fantasy of superfluity is payback for the horrific regularity of the experience of limit. Which is real? Is my breast real, which cousins language, transistor from which the energy you need for life—for the bicycling legs, the fretting, the focus—can be drawn?

*Wednesday, 16 July 2008*

## GOOD INTENTIONS

Two external sockets arbitrate
for everyone's call to begin. Buzzing and shorted,
the supply backs up to the catastrophic
overflow managed by a wizard mouse
or Chaplin's chocolate-chew mouth.
She takes control of your fantasy,
and you try to make slow
a desire for recovery and plainness.
Later a cyborg, pinioned to tubes.
You thought to return but the purchase
is not that easy: you suborn variety
in a vast field full of white paintings,
and think it moral to take
another measure. Silence in cream.
To hold the view alone
with tenderness, that this spark
prevents her immediate extinction;
you hold that thought, and don't break her
drunk sleep puffed out with her
own organic charms. Drunk with power
the agency has allocated to you a set of limited
functions: basis of your new
ethics, a syllabus that flows,
life reduced to a brute composition,
to tarry, dreamy, let slip deep
into your bagged and sloping body
please present to the counter
when your number
is called.


These are your activities. We've just laid you in nothing but
your nappy on the antiqued bed, where you lie on your side,
arms crossed and shoulders bare. The calm vulnerability of a
post-coital sleeper, I can almost see into the secrets of your

adult life. Spent, I held you through the night against nurse's instructions, both of us wrapped in towelling like swimmers on shingle: one of us had panted and strained, oxen, the other compressed as a bean, and now we collapse into the shocked concavity of our struggle. Our total intimacy can't last, must embarrass you into exploration. But for now here you are, against the cool enormity of my skin, safe and voracious.

*17 August 2008, Castellina*

Raising from cries to babble to speech. But also *lowering*: lying down beside her, am low in agonies as I push her uphill on these obsolete and offensive stirrups. I bring all my disciplines to bear the empty space and the complex cacophony of newly being through which she finds her way: we return every day to the same proscriptions. Relieving myself of the mania of progress, for her sake. Being occupied. *Low*, the moaning, mooing noise of relief and comfort, of milk-making.

Awake with perpetual fluorescence in the cheerful squalor of the postnatal ward, I remember Rilke's injunction: 'One must have memories of many nights of love, none of which was like the others, of the screams of women in labour, and of light, white, sleeping women in childbed, closing again.' I can't sleep because I want to watch my child and am shocked by the violence of her production; I'm not closing, becoming something white and veiled, but continuing to open like a fountain. This is my justification. For a writing of honest particularity, not clean, in a form which would catch rather than cauterize this pouring.

*30 March 2009*

Yesterday your first laugh. Small and gathered only in the mouth, the white reveal in your bottom gum, painful thread of your tongue tie, animal tip of your tongue: laugh sparks here instantly and seeps away. I was using your fist to pat your cheek and punch the air. Repetition and predictability. You still don't like to see us too close, a kiss or clench makes you screech or at the very least you blink in consternation those tearless eyes. Joy then is learnt, adaptive, where sorrow bursts open immediately. But you laughed: you are enjoying us.

What am I doing here? Where is the model of duplicity for the kind of writing I want to make for you, and of you? Your laughter reminds me that you are an audience, contorting us into performances. I just go a bit farther, so far, than you do, but it means less to me: my habits are formed.

*29 August 2008*

The tiny midwife with her ginger hair, cap and heavy boots, palpitates my stomach and reports that it is still just 'at the brim'. Head was still down, pivot of a new world, ready to tumble in danger and courage of thinking straight into the air. And to make of that air a warm human embrace.

You're emerging from deep sleep now; your heel has been pricked, new blurry sweller, you gave just one bright, damaged cry as I pushed my breast down on you to try to keep you from all harm, even the harm of benefit. I will have to learn many things, including how to be reconciled to all the disasters you need.

*Monday, 23 June 2008*

Harsh, ragged objects were concealed,
    Oppressions, tears and cries,
Sins, griefs, complaints, dissentions, weeping eyes,
  Were hid: and only things revealed
Which heavenly spirits and the angels prize.
    The State of Innocence
  And Bliss, not trades and poverties,
    Did fill my sense.

Now you're ill again. We came to admonish you in your cot and found you in a bib of purple vomit; then a fountain of lunch, blueberry and lamb with sweet potatoes and mango poured into my trouser cuffs. Soaked over and over again, your head in a helmet of gut juices, sick streaming out of your nose to leave you with two sooty nostrils and the sneezes. I take you up for a bath, we splash around obliviously, motes of breakfast shadowing the bed of the tub. Three days like this, you cry it up again, milk in great geysers overflowing the grown-up bed. We wash you, your head slick and your eyes half-closed with dreamy confusion like the mucky neonate. My breasts get heavier and heavier with unused nurture. The muslins stink like baker's whites.

*20 April 2009*

# SPOONERIZED

The job is finished, the job again.

                    Moving forward
to repress the move sideways. Rocking
to iron the shout. The window you notice
doubles as an exit. To hover in gentleness
sometimes coronal: another horror show
an archaeology of the overcome. Bays.

Suddenly then you switch off, the hyperbole
trickles down a drain necking inclined towards
bitten porcelain. I can get through
the irrigation ditch on my knees
and hands are retractable to the plainness
of sleeves, no rocket in them.

Eyeball the ordinance
beacon to turn you into a cast form. Abra,
abstracted, your livid twisting
attribute of matter as a proportionality
stripped down to mere extension.
Adapted to a likeable sphere
where air happens to be see-through.

Your cries concatenate into noughts
and ones and triplets and finish
tails. Drip-dry
everything down to a piece of blank
information: make this the space
for love, love's echo chamber.


On Monday cries of steep and bottomless pain, arc of your
back a rictus of muscular suffering, your round head pulled
into a red decanter. You choked on the heal-all, becoming
aware that life entails a renunciation of relief.

A trip to the Tate, when suddenly you became a rooting, snuffling and griping consumer in the Cy Twombly exhibit, made me worry for my own liberation. I was naff, bungling breast-pads, shooting milk over your shoulder onto the parquet, giving paintings a soundtrack of pig grunts and squalid hunger. And once you were latched on, thinking: it won't be that easy, though the scrawls on the chapel wall point to regression as an exit. Then you slept, the bony nodule on your chest levitating in dream and heat, all the long bus journey from London Bridge on a bed of wool, and ease re-entered the margins. Now you're coming down the hallway in M's arms, red-faced, your sleep gown smelling of olive oil and yourself in the 26 degrees.

*Saturday, 26 July 2008*

The morning nap, the second cup of tea. Species stroll in the garden. Gratefulness.

Not reading so much these days as devouring. Leap from page to page, scavenging for the point. Stuff it in my gob, then, usually, forget it.

The quick quick quick of your rest times: get the washing in, the cutlery to its coffins, tidy and oblige. Getting through the tasks. Using up the day. Then the slow, the slow of feeding you. We linger until the nipple falls from your mouth, and I can feel a slight shift of weight in your head. Then listen with fear for the end of my furlough: might I not have time to say and do, quick quick quick.

Learn in all to economize. And lavishly to spend.

*12 March 2009*

# DISSENT

Counting the year in wash tabs, in kilos
of white fat and brown. I upbraid the
    kitchen
though it serves my desires. We cook
    you up,
knowing the chemistry is irreversible
and the past evaporates under any sky:
harming you into being, survivably
    indifferent.

To cook an egg imperfectly. To solder
the remedies which have nothing to do
    with that
into a shape like a helmet. I fit it
under my top. I can throw over
this whole house a grid ordered
on repeat from my usual suppliers,
and it will count everything against a
    pain clicker.

This is the holding order, as we hold
the outrageous truths of the future
against you, a state of confusion which
    doubles
their tenacity into an obsession: not
    remembering
the first time I learnt about murder, it
becomes now the meat sore, around which
play wraps a layer of sweet health.

Some day you will be inducted, and the
    ragged
object flying before your eyes
kaleidoscope in blood the material you
    knew.
But you'll see nothing new. You started out
a creature of trade: you get your best terms,
fight your poverty with greed and violent
    sound.

Until you can state yourself I would be lying
if I left you alone with the angels.
It's easier to make a house a charnel
than to represent us together,
swimming under the sign for joy.

What is the function of this text? Where does it go? You skim
along my skin, electric in my nerve endings, so why do I need
to remember you in translation? Reading backwards, I am
reminded of the detail of being with you, and being yours,
and you being who you are, inscrutable, incipient. How many
details I have already forgotten in the exactitude of your pre-
sentness. When I tell people about what I'm doing they cast
around politely (dejectedly?), recommend a postpartum doc-
ument. Every discovery has its concept. But what if the

note—record of zeal overflowing—sponges off your initiate life? Narcissism parading as detail, looking both ways before crossing the troubled line between domesticity and action, home and writing, lines which up till now have felt too dangerously electrified even to approach. The chronic absenteeism of a political critique must have its letter.

But not to dwell in you, on it, would be an act of penance, of asceticism. These are not the kind of words I stand up for in burgled cafes. 'To admire and want. To want to say, but feel chagrin for obvious saying, but to be urgent, defying, pinning together and sewing, to be ripping apart and wiping, to be cooking soup and typing, ... but to choose a desk and a chair and to feel the singleness of it, the actual child of it coming home', Kathleen Fraser writes. I come up with excuses, absolving home of its monasticism. Certainly I don't want to *do that*, to turn the euphoria into a product for knowledge. But if I wonder how to persuade anyone that the writing of infancy is a cause for truths overlooked by first philosophies, those Christmas pageants for grown men, surely the first question is, whom am I persuading? Not you. There's no reason for you to regard my colonization of your beginnings as anything other than an intrusion, and an excruciating record of unbearable intimacy, sexless body pressed against body. From the moment of your birth, you have been slowly wriggling away. Eventually you will find the idea of me practically disgusting.

*28 January 2009*

Is love ever progressive, if all happiness is just a fragment of the entire happiness people are denied? Is love for you a fragment? An opening or a hoarding? In my finest spirits it feels like the reply to alienation, a new spring neighbours wouldn't dare fight to soil or siphon. So much work is contracted to an assurance of the inescapability of unhappiness. In the livery of catastrophe it seeks the temporary pleasures of *energeia* as release. Our souls can move, through a feudal kingdom, and the poet courts the reader as the one person who might understand and agree with his otherwise close prisoning. The reader (the beloved) is scorned by the general, feasted by the particular. Our fabled consensus is an aggravated defence against public shame.

On Christmas Eve, in the blue liquidity of lights and gifts in static manufactured wonder, M reads me a friend's poem, which puzzles the reality of the desire to give. That desire shows the boundaries of creativity, policed by the fetish and irrecuperable failures to overcome it: made in China, bought with credit, typical and passable and extreme in the limits it endorses. But the objects ring out from their altars in the display case, promising continuation beyond the fragility of poor crude lives. The poem has no idea how to break their spell. So family itself becomes a mystical attribute, more miniature gods static in memory and far-off, decking the hearth and 'the warm kitchen table'. The poem is thinking about the family on the edge of the city, between the fields and the sodium polish of the shopping district. Its honourable finitude is an antidote to the infinity of objects we might bring home in tribute, and to the finitude of the thinking which chooses one for each. How far away, how opaque and solid and fuzzy are 'my child' and 'my wife': the goods which belong, by other means. But I see the present and though its tinsel qualities infuse me with a foreboding of your eventual death I miss you (you upstairs sleeping noisily) intensely as the person to whose pleasure it is consecrated. I miss a humane account of the household, of friendship, paracosms that prevent our utter ruination.

*21 January 2010*

## CENTRAL AIR

Models of the red ace stall to dance
up the rotary display unit. It is like a screw,
that nails modernity to the asphalt, and leads
laughing hyenas to twist
their grins into vacuity. Human life converted
    into flow past stations of confused colour,
      thinking into a cowry shell. An inter-
mission to the hocus city, baked to a crisp
and grossly full and grossly historical
it resists all compromise and is a work
against nature, where 'nature' signifies
    the city itself as the foolish
    durability of the static.
We are tourists to a violence of plenty
that scrolls through Macy windows, and stays open
and doesn't fold when we bolt out. We talked about it,
and our plans were manifold.

And our play is folding, leaf on leaf, gathering
fine print the technicalities of commitment,
information gathering as deep cover for luck;
folding water over, to bring to the surface
the fossilized or the original, to introduce them
in a healing exhibition
               to the accidental,
               the wrong, the newly struck.
    Our ideas may have no
durability;          their standing is a coin float,
             their beauty the diagram in sweet blood
        where they track and cross, wait, inch or drop.

'Does the household obey an idea?'
The book of nature is pigmented oils called the house.
It is one of the few on this plot without engineered air;
pervious, it presents its dream face to the ocean
and its night-and-day face to the thrusting air.

Though somewhat lacking in the soft furnishings
of sleep it is rigorous as it bends and takes. Inside it is
a portrait, and menageries of livings—
fish, sheep and pig called 'bear'. Inside
the buckling ocean seen:

1.     from the dull shingle of Hastings, sadly;
2.     lit by unnatural fire, at Lycian tombs;
3.     foraging for bright arthropods over coconut shallows;
4.     managed, where the combers prowl;
5.     interzonal, and as metaphor bisected by a golden thread

that brings us back to life. These collations
like hatch marks on the wash, gather stories into
a single feed: two, then three, lives wandering,
                    not without hint of force, not without heat
                    that could scar if it doesn't first raise the miniature corn
                    beyond expectations; not always inclined,
                    hardly perfect, sometimes single, sometimes in pairs,
                    sometimes dozy and often scientists, filling the green
                    cup with water, to test flow,
                    texture of a necessity which we trust with our lives
                    though it might tumble us to oblivion.

And the wind is a fable that the earth breathes.
And the belly of waters
which wobbles when it walks the earth
is a shift in the zone of fathomless plenty.
Is just density, shifting back and forth among the shores
who share it and share the spectators in double orbit.
Is the trinity trying to empty the sea with a seashell,
is conflict so endlessly repeated it becomes play.
Is a kind of sharing. Gathers the most unforgiving
materials, and softens them
to fit in exactly those cups.


Where are the models for writing about babies, rather than getting
babies to help us write about ourselves? Too few love lyrics for the

babies as the babies are. Too much mirroring: *specula naturae*, cup of wishes, fountain of memories, when you are elsewhere, covered in sweet corn and braying until my life splits into two narratives, one a soap opera that dumps me in the county jail, the other some horrid Bill Viola film, I'm an actor slowed down in stupid khaki. Too few love lyrics for individual children. Too many poems that mourn and celebrate the birth of the self. Too few love lyrics for the babies as the babies are. In 'Frost at Midnight', the poet is alongside 'my cradled infant', who, but for his breathing, seems less alive than the stranger in the grate. That 'film' is the 'sole unquiet thing', sympathetic companion with 'me who live'. Is the infant not also included with 'me' in life? Hartley's breathing, the speech of his sleep, fills up the 'interspersèd vacancies / And momentary pauses of the thought': is *between* thinking. What could the baby lend to thought? Ayla is the beginning of that thought which starts from her. She does her own thing, is proud.

No adult relation would stand still long enough to sustain this kind of scrutiny. She can't crawl yet or fend for her own food, so I get to watch her: who has been indecipherable, and read in the middle of sirens.

*30 March 2009, Aberystwyth*

Why is it reassuring to believe that you do not begin in thought but only in feeling? Rousseau: '*Les premières sensations des enfans sont purement affectives; ils n'appercoivent que le plaisir et la douleur*'—or Prynne: 'The babe, when it comes to its mother's breast, / takes the milk and thrives, it does not search / for the root and well-spring from which it / flows so. It sucks the milk and empties / the whole measure'. The infant is no philologist, just a primary consumer of the unsymbolized. But watch her latch on, prowling by instinct towards the scent: animal mystery, how she recognizes nourishment as a specific tag within the barrage of totally new visuality. Denise Riley: 'A blind baby feeling for the breast knows the taste of milk'. The taste is already in the mouth, as a memory, and a primordial language. In the hot welter of all this information, the inauguration of sense, she sniffs and follows. At last she has an object for the skill practiced for months on brine. When the milk lets down I feel it as lines, a carbolic net, my machine-body giving it up to the little pig who knows what she's doing. Show of the gradual. Unlearnt capacities from two degrees of life: one ancient, one modern.

*8 July 2010*

Sometimes it is thin and blue. Sometimes it comes so quick, after the stinging nettles open, that you look around to avoid choking. You must stay for the thick bit, the rich calorific end. A milky dialectic. For the first six months of life, even when those thick wrists with their pin-line creases had outgrown the first sleeves, there was nothing to you that had not come through my body, tho' I wasn't poor.

*12 December 2008*

We move through the valley and find image after image of milk. Everywhere we go the *Madonna del Latte* opens her heavy dress to the privilege of the child's mouth. The breast detaches itself and points towards the heavenly bow. Sometimes she pinches it, her constrictive fingers doubling as a blessing. The Galaktotrophousa, her unclamped breast lifted in a bowl. Clement of Alexander argued that she merely seeped liquid flesh, a passive vessel for the divine food. In paintings, Christ sits upright on her throne-lap, gets a cricked neck: the twist in the fat baby body shows he's oriented against realism towards mankind, not the passion of nourishment dripping from his columnar mother. To drink is to surrender the dynamism of outwardness but this child is never distracted from his blessings and reforms. So his perfect feast generates no resentment.

At night, as the noise of snuffling greed is suppressed in a dark bedroom, Bernard de Clairvaux licks his lips.

*20 August 2008, Castellina*

The cleft of your chin to take after M: your face rumbles up to the beard, the kiss a possible threat, biting, snapping off, scratching. Desire is consumptive, consumption is an anger mixed with lust as incorporation. It is the fantasy of maceration as an erasure of limits. Through dancing play in which we are interchangeable, eater and eaten, belly and banquet, you test the limits of personhood on the dental line: I can still hear the scrape of ceramic knives.

Your short case of foot and mouth. Despite the refrain of 'ot, ot', with a pneumatic expression, we carried you out, took you to the pound. You gave up my milk last Tuesday: your lip with a pasting of ulcer turned down against the expectation of pain. Repetition sours a primitive history of delight. I read that among the Kaliai nursing is meant to continue until the child is able to recount its dreams or can gather shellfish. On 4 October, fifteen months old, that intimate dance stumbles and ends, with no inkling of your dreams or how your economic life will begin.

*12 October 2009*


Your first dream: you are stuck on rocks, in rock pools, and I come to collect you in a hot-air balloon. This is a panic inspired by crabs. Your second dream: you are diving through deep water which is full of 'creatures', limpets and jellyfish and starfish. For a long time you claimed to dream about whales but that was probably flattery. You dream of sharks, and sniffing anteaters and a spider swelling over the room. Of abandonment and reintroduction: making do with your singularity, under stress. Mostly you are confused, asking to return to the swings, the sea, the porous border between sleeping and waking for you no analogue.

*12 February 2011*


Your skin flaking, legacy of your amphibian life. Though we smooth oils over, white flakes of your old self drift over the bed, our clothes, the air, supply us with dust. Already in decay; also sloughing the old world away, declaring your independence of the past: *exitus à morte*.

The breast continues to deliver, though its power is waning, eclipsed by the expanding three dimensions of a mobile world. You twist immediately in the confusion of holding to get back down, to hit the road, touch the outer atmosphere where windows pattern the enormity of 'outside' into consumable squares. Unless the blind is drawn and the mood gently negative, you're not content to lie around. I try to keep it up, pumping milk alongside your itineracy, but you don't like that plastic sibling, a Dr Seuss bamplooza, inert and iconic and annoying. You cry and whine as you try to peel it off me, to suck your property out of the grotesque mouth of the funnel. You are on notice: you have been born into a world of machines.

*17 May 2009*

# 2

He is purely happy, because he knows no evil, nor hath made means by sin to be acquainted with misery. He arrives not at the mischief of being wise, nor endures evils to come, by foreseeing them. He kisses and loves all, and, when the smart of the rod is past, smiles on his beater. Nature and his Parents alike dandle him, and 'tice him on with a bait of sugar to a draught of wormwood . . . Could he put off his body with his little coat, he had got eternity without a burthen, and exchanged but one Heaven for another.

John Earle, *Microcosmographie*

When you wake in the dark you call with no vibrato, so we let ourselves wait it out. The monitor's lights tremble and surge like the equalizer for your doubtful permanence. If you are sleeping it steadies itself on the single green bar, the background noise of vitality, we press it and hear the faint intake and outflow of your continuing. That sonic pulse of a distant star. Your smallness a trick of perspective, light from a distance the single clue to your composition, hanging in the thick of all that space, but also in good company. Worlds revolve round you and are busied with noise and itineraries, and you are held aloft—as the old universe was—by care.

*11 May 2009*


You are adept at pointing. We're so thrilled by communicative gestures that we obey our rider, follow the ray of light that extends from finger to object: old-fashioned roller, chiming can. Your feet outrun you as we pinion you upright and move you around the room like a hoover. You reach the ball and turn it under your foot with surprising nimbleness. You wave. You pull my locks and raven for my nose, grotesque face-centred nipple you chew and shout over; the hair at my temples is now short-cropped from pulling. You eat everything.

But the content of all days and nights is the same. You wake repeatedly in paroxysms of disaster, nothing but feeding would coax you back. Was it headache, toothache; was it spiritual? Should we tough-love you into submission, or to solicit your emotional health, feed it, usher it past? In the end we did what we always do, talk about it, fail to understand, cope and pass. Always responding to emergencies, not forming, not making except by accident and by a general theory of kindness. To go on caring for you, with the fullest repertoire of movements and sounds.

*29 April 2009*

Expert witnesses school us to routinize you out of your dependence on our embraces, teach you to sleep alone, soothe yourself. Make you a regular feeder: a good stock animal. 'What is an infant but a brute beast in the shape of a man?' Hide lineaments of milk. But as you want to be held so I want to press you as we ride waves of interrupted urban sleep together. To con you out of waking to the noise of truck work, to lock you in a monogamous gaze, irresistible watch on the origins of day. At the end of pregnancy I would get up early, toddle on a ball like a big seal and watch the light come up as background to wheeling birds: quiet, abiding as practice and preserve. Now, the whole night acquires a new structure, its constancy in profile against big blind screens of endurance. You and me, we can't indulge the fantasy of surpassing, sleeping from light to light like tight pillars of joy. The trash, the disorder, persist on a gradient which we can measure by quantity of a round. So the whole day shifts. This isn't an experience of peace, dozing through the evolution of the watches; but it is the end of that peculiar desire, the head asleep as soon as it hits, the image of resurrection.

So disoriented, we get susceptible. If we don't follow orders we are threatened with punishment. But more severe is the fear of losing you, the slack bond to the fading face. You will be beautiful every day, growing in interest as in capacity, but I grieve for your plenum of joyful repetition, hurrying into the dissolution for which we still have no script. 'All Time was Eternity, and a perpetual Sabbath. Is it not strange, that an infant should be heir to the whole world, and see those mysteries which the books of the learned never unfold?' Elated, often tearful, prone to idealize as the counterweight of my losses. Regularly mystified even by the small palette of your needs, how to arrange the satisfactions.

*Wednesday, 16 July 2008*

It helps to fall asleep
in the same condition you will rouse to.
It helps to fall asleep
braced against the tumid and massive presence
of the feeder, the custodian of your needs.
She marks time she and the day
is long the same things keep happening
is it out yet yes
like a light, glowing hot. We put you down
in a cage, that comes with these instructions:
fearful loneliness is the condition
of your liberation, and will yield to pleasure
if not to horror and a dry mouth.


And last night I got to sleep again, in the day bed, and despite
the racing heartbeat that scorns my breaking fatigue. Because
I decamped, with M, in need of local warmth and compan-
ionate breath. Why shouldn't you be the same?

Meanwhile, in the thick of your sleeplessness, of my three
days of sleeplessness, momentarily I can't recognize you. I
come home from work, your skin is browner, your eyes a dif-
ferent shape in your head. You look older. Is your hair styled?
I sat in the supervision room, thinking of something I want
to tell M but I pictured us in the old house, rested, eating and
drinking, co-locating ourselves in complaint and joy and our
fields and mysteries. I put you out of it. This makes me a bit
nauseous but, of course, ambivalences are part of it. I can
hardly believe you never hate me.

*29 April 2009*


insomnia insomnia insomnia

*11 November 2008, 5 a.m.*

Again the middle of the night. Bed no refuge, the heartbeat quickens to pinpoints on the discovery that I'm asleep: wake up, toss, breathe. To accommodate your rhythms I've lost my pace by night: and sit in the kitchen contemplating spaces made cavernous by insomnia. So then this is the space earned, compensation for myself as extra? You wake when we go up, crying us back beyond all electronic aid. Enough of this and I've got an adrenaline heap, raised each time I'm nearly drifting and you begin to cry again, airing your complaints in your desultory way.

*27 May 2009*

Striped wild with watching the hills
have no use for personality and make it
known. These are the engines
of continuance, the passion to wake
perpetually making a use of time: the stars
emptying to pasture, the radiant child
unappeasable in her needs, the husband
disapparl'd of neat counting. I cannot lie
still in my hunger for it, the future
as continuation of this absolute present,
or heave back down this heart
on its panic of flex. It's too much wanting
when all hope is in process
of satisfying: so says the child,
unimpressed by the straight-lined air,
and as she cedes to sleep doubling
over on itself I am a slave to succession:
to inhabit the passing time without fear,
and so to lose it, to give over the night's
vanguard formation in ice and sharply-
drawn reality, is the sickness revealed
only in the manic chalking of the forerunners.

**INSOMNIAD 2** *HOME, 12 January 2011, 12.30 a.m.*

Turning it over, the body warm with complacency,
her appealing neck signed for an
apparent breach sealed with a solution
who is not transparent. We know things about
the other body behind the door
we can't allude to, it sinks into
even the in-out pattern of our sleeping.
How much the lime leaf is a relic of isolation
putting on a show in the park, with the palsied twig
gross even by today's standards
she holds out against cruelty.
Except for the passion of my standing by,
holding the sails of the transport bag,
it would be a catastrophe, in all the papers.
Except we divide up
the treasure in the hallway, with the man
smiling his entrance, providing another brace of
unspeakable relations.

The heart is grounded, like a sideboard
over which servants show their concern
as duty paid in moving machinery
the hazard there in the invisible catches.
It is of me and nothing of me.
Estranged by repetition which becomes constancy
in the way disease does, its terrible fecundity.
I act as if nothing's happening. The sliding
doors rattle but the contents are lumpish.
Though I can feel that this fantasy
will look as petty as a dream speech
in the retrospect of reclamation,
as glassy as a thought is, having been
the world before it, I am no fool
for the rigour of my own affirmations:
stalked by negatives, stiff as a hand,
the carapace of my fiction
is polished and shining like the black branches
picked out by the neighbouring
security light, individual, frequent,
hard, immobile, terrifying, capillary.
No future but repetition of the darkest:
this is the endless thought I am ill to believe in.

**INSOMNIAD 4** *27 January 2011, 10.30 p.m.*

Fussbudget: you flatter and court sleep
like a wood louse on a bouncy castle, clipping
static in the marathon for ultimate rest.
The sensation eludes you, a learnt punishment
where the other anxieties, displaced, can be
dipped. A force to stop. Guilt erupts
like cockatiel acne, thoughts of breakfast
and the orange juice of mothering, and then
rage, at the slept voices of radio, the city full
of compartments where sleep is joyfully a bath
and so ignored, and then deep loneliness,
out and ionized on a wire. What the newborn
baby knows, after the electricity of passage
has been switched off: what anyone does on trains.
Or maybe in the newborn's incredible eye,
searching the hospital scenic for an explanation,
there is something like that impulse,
to make sense of the wildness by nerve
mistaken for rational cogitation. In the night I say
the man is a pillar, his hand made of gigantic carrots,
the curse is waves breaking against the glass,
and still don't recognize this as the beginning
of the pleasure I believe will come
only to those who seduce it with magic rituals,
valerian, pins and theoretical hammocks.

You drift over the speed bumps of sleep. A ghostly child comes singing through the monitor. I am so stupidly in thrall to narrative that I've snuck into your room, goaded by whispers, imagining a hag bent over your cot, scratching you with her bony finger: or a prowler half through the window, shushing you into his checked bag. If we were to disappear completely now, how long would a trace of us remain for you?

These past few days have felt perilous. The cornice of a proper tooth pierces your gum, pitting the pink ridge with vicious indestructibility. Are the teeth making you jumpy? The carnivore emerges. The dog, the snake. All ferocity is born from weakness, according to Seneca—but weakness is not a condition you were born with, you have had to learn it, as a mode of comparison of yourself to other creatures (including your own creature, imagination). So you were in paroxysms of fear at the sound of the food processor, whizzing your chicken into gummable pellets. You cry when I knocked you back for pinching my nipple, ravenous beyond hunger, in the tuck of the fur. Yesterday M stood below, trying to kiss you goodbye; you dodged the scrape of his face on your brief skin, and kept trying to bury yourself in my shoulder, until he seized one on you that made your face screw into pantomime disaster. But imagine, child, the long days and nights, the way you folded up in his arms at your birth, the blooming lunar movements of your newborn limbs, like sea plants waving: walking you, coveting you, all the days of your life.

*6 May 2009*

Damaged week. You woke screaming two nights ago, your face beetroot-red and puffy. We took you to the out-of-hours GP, then the misery of the late-night A&E. You were brilliantly curious with your puffball head, and fell asleep around 2 a.m. in the glare of the wards. When it was our turn at last I flopped you onto the paper bed, to sprawl wide and loose as the doctor looked you over. That panic that turned me into a 'hysterical harpy' according to M: tales of mysterious rashes that become septicaemia, the tumbler test, a wasp in your bed?

*22 April 2009*

A new vista opens among us. Though you are far off from 'getting sense', here you've been naughty, refusing to eat your dinner, refusing your second and your chair. Your strength in recalcitrance is impressive. We explain that it makes us sad when you don't eat your dinner. You put one hand on either side of my neck and press, gently. Then do this, single hand by single hand, to M's neck. Despite this kindness we make no progress, and eventually begin the punishment regime for the first time. I carry you to the step, and hold your thighs in place as you scream and writhe on the gridiron. The impulse to calm you down, pushing you back from disintegration, is strong but there's a lesson here and a feeling we are all under surveillance. We have a second go. This time you agree to sit in your chair. I say, good girl, thank you. You say, 'Mama happy. Dada happy. Ayla happy too.' After we read about Murdoch the train, and you are very keen to add that Murdoch happy, and Murdoch no happy, as the cartoon face requires. Shuddering. Our group solidarity is dependent first on the discipline whose profit is happiness as conformity.

*14 July 2010*

'In South American Piaroa society, which totally disallows the display of physical violence and where children are never physically punished, the play is accompanied by very little dissension or anger.' To bring you to gentleness, must we exclude anger and violence from your world, until you're old enough to contain it within a complex shell of the already-made? Children who hit in the park, they seem to know a different lesson. It's impossible to consider the news reports now without recognizing a hideous proximity, how quickly the immense gift of our ability to sustain life can curdle into its opposite: mortal authority. I push down red floods wherever they rise up, but does all childcare include controlled sadism? Anger and violence are already inside me, learnt capacities which can't be scoured from the past. Are they already inside you, an electrical system on unstable pause? Does the figure of the angry child, the depressive or psychotic child, live with the modern taint of unrelieved sin? Or, does believing that you are immaculate of it shut down your possibilities, keep under a terrible guard one of the things which makes you human enough to be loved?

*6 January 2009*

I don't have much time, of course; and no retreat. I can't occupy the poem in process of building it. I'm taking notes on what is happening somewhere else. Memomiranda. Fragments ruin my surety, the poem's poise and precocity as it makes meaning in the making: I don't have that kind of time anymore. The meaning has already been made, on the flower-printed blanket, with the floppy lamb, the melting spoon, the Perspex boxes of tricks for eye and ear. The poem is our joint encounter with the pane of glass, the sudden shot of birds from the rooftops: the ineluctable modality of the visible. I try to hold onto it long enough to carry to the car, to the table.

How can I translate your instinctive grammar, plaintive, joyful, angry, needful, radiantly calling, full in everything but a tense structure, into the wishful operations of a poem? In a late essay 'On the Sense of Loneliness', Melanie Klein describes the desire to return to the perfect communication of mother and infant: 'However gratifying it is in later life to express thoughts and feelings to a congenial person, there remains an unsatisfied longing for an understanding without words', for the preverbal communication of infant with mother. The legacy of this unsatisfied longing is nothing more or less than the integration of the infant ego. Its legacy in writing is the endless repetition of the deferral of satisfaction.

*30 March 2009*

Now you're chewing on your hand, searching for the thumb that refuses to disengage the cavity of fingers. You're just beginning to realize that you can satisfy yourself, achieve the pleasure of orality with only the equipment of your body. You slurp greedily and inefficiently. Also more fretful. On Tuesday you had your first injection. It was the worst thing that had ever happened to you. A matter-of-fact paediatrician dug under your marbled skin with the needle, finding a just spot in its incarnate crease. You howled angrily as you were held down, exposed to the brutality of preventative justice. We prove your life as an accumulation of distributed harms.

*29 August 2008*

We move house, M returns to work; you wake up, M takes you downstairs, he returns you and you sleep shortly, sidled to my breast. We play together, you gripe, you are rolled out and sleep covered, parked in the back room. You wake so disastrously quickly, or sleep so dangerously long. The afternoon unravels. The day closes. I press you to stay a bit longer, the bath helps to divert you from the pain of wakefulness, you scream the house down as I tuck mitts on your sausages.

This is the routine, guarantor of your happiness and emblem of my knowledge of you: of how to operate you. The nights are less predictable. As you surface and sink, the mitts go crackling all over your dear face. Eczema is dreadful. I had to drag the bed into our unfinished room on election day, because I couldn't lie awake listening to those mitts going and going. Now I'm running bewildered into your room four times a night to gather you up before you're beset by complete terror. The breast makes it so all right that you shudder and pant while I'm preparing it. The need is terrifying, a clear addiction.

All this means what it says in books: the decline of any other kind of intimacy. Disappearance of intellectual ambition. Invisibility of domestic labour. All time is stolen from you, sneaking up the stairs and hoping the giant won't realize we've absconded with the loot: a newspaper, the telephone, the language.

> Is the yeare onely lost to me?
>> Have I no bayes to crown it?
> No flowers, no garlands gay? All blasted?
>> All wasted?
> Not so, my heart: but there is fruit,
>> And thou hast hands.

Sometimes I resent that something which possesses you. As I did on Saturday night, but came to find you on Sunday morning, like an admonition, smiling and kicking with excitement in your cot to see me and see the day: your face covered in blood. An icing of blood on the rim of your sleeping bag, a stained sheet under your cheek. You'd pulled a huge patch of skin off your right cheek in your sleep, captured by the ecstasy of scratching.

So it's all as difficult as it is supposed to be, and I get no help, and I am solely responsible, and my work—the tidying, the washing, the drying, the watching and propping and applauding is all invisible, and the real work vanishes into thin air, I can't read or write. M has retreated to the top floor to sleep after another useless argument comparing our deprivations, my cheeks crusty with anger. And yet. What I will lose and how I will not improve by the time we are together—these things are themselves substitutes for the longed-for and absent thing, the qualities of visceral, immediate, passionate joy, as I watch you, my daughter, learn to lift your head.

*10 November 2008*

# THE EEL STATION

1.

J. G. A. Pocock has moved on
through the history
of the world from antiquity
to enlightenment, and the panels
twitch on the frequency of revelation
as antidote to the republic
slippery in Macedonia and
corroded in Rome. A worker
is singing her broom up
the hallway, her language
I will let her sleep on for this to be able
I distracted that scene in M*A*S*H
where it's revealed to the tolerant intellectual
that Hawk-eye persuaded the woman
on the felted bus to smother
her child rather than her chicken.
The chicken felted the squawk
the child made the dark to, ring to,
the parable is sociality as the ultimate
sacrifice as the clerics smile
kindly with self-awareness.
And my arms form an open cell
stir the vacuum all this life,
lanced by the mute inglorious pirate
under the sofa, his obscene pecker,
his unremovable hat and unrecoverable
topos eye. They the arms reach under
the skin. The cheek is full and resonantly hard,
movement and rebellion showing the organism
is still robust: these would be the pressures,
temperatures, spaces and containments
I most would struggle to remember
how moving on to anything

this thought a remote vengeance of the work,
but no, instead the thought of how evasive she is
wakes me for water, for the blind,
for the reassuring noises coming
from the man speaking into his hat.

2.

The bathroom of Gravers Lane
with its subway tiles gives onto college,
and four of them at the door,
a double pair, *paar,*
*schreib mir ein paar Zeilen,*
bang bang bang then throttle.
I'm trying to get cleaned up here
but the water overflows the edges
and the edges are overflowed with claret,
thick and thin cassia, wormcase,
then the worms themselves, black braided
rope the thickness of a pencil and
coming out signally to swim.
The portrait of Elizabeth recovered
a snake coiling like an entrance
in her fruit-basket hand. So these
ropes up until the point
that I realize I have a coronet
a circlet a rush wicket an eclipse
of them with the sticker from Homebase
shoved in the indeterminacy
and duly it comes down. Hang on
I'm ready OK I'm coming out now. The four
undergraduates are boisterous in the way
and I've done the tub,
but I look back and the tiles
my Jupiter legs the amphora the void
between the ears of the radiator,
you guessed it.

3.

This field of blood is not finished
but sacrificed in blind faith
and fills a coronet days with dying.
We don't like to say so
but there it is. Over
we go through it again.
Choughs, and rooks brought forth
for all the famous potentiality
the life-stuff the tenderizer
this primitive accumulation then
potlatch takes us closer to death
as a population of our life.
Sometimes used to clear a field:
this is called a pig tractor.
I'm not saying it isn't necessary,
just that this is in the code
for freedom.

The chitchat, the blather. The talk in the cot, the potter. Your first complex sentence is a command, unsurprisingly: 'No Mama eat Ayla toast!' We sing 'Old McDonald had a farm', and you supply animals. Then you supply tractor, and crab and then people: Mama and Dada, with a 'no' here and a 'no' there! But this reflection of our endless negativity is then corrected—the social instinct to flatter—to 'happy'.

And tonight as I put you down you are full of language. 'Mama close window, bit quiet! Dark. Ayla in dark. Ayla bit quiet in dark. Mama hold hand. Mama hold Mapmap hand. Ayla *nightmare*. Ayla dream about crab. Ayla foot in sea. Cold! Sea dark. Dark car park—*nightmare*. Ayla dream about Ayla dinner! Ayla sit in chair. Ayla dream about eat dinner. Ayla sit in other chair—naughty chair, no! Ayla eat lollipop. Mmmmm! Cold. Don't drop lollipop (*laughs at her own rhyme*). Mama close window, bit quiet! Ayla poo-ah. Ayla poo-ah in dark. Poo-ah come out, play. Dada no wear Ayla hat. Mama check! Poo-ah in dark. Mama change nappy. Mama put poo-ah away. Mama and Dada put poo-ah in bin! Night in dark. Quiet in dark. Ayla cold in night, Mama close window, bit quiet! Shoe tight. Ayla wake up, Ayla talkin'. Mama sing Ayla other chair, lalalalala. Mama come back!'

So I leave you with these consolations, the story about the ha-ha, the window and the park, then: 'Mama close window, bit quiet. Ayla close eyes.' And then you're silent and we are suspended all night in the tenderness of what you've told us.

*24 July 2010*

## RESONANCE DREAMING

We are not asleep, as contours press
against the shallow drape; birds are not,
and lightly communicating down
silver wires. Ayla is mostly asleep, rising
from a rescue action in the rock pools to churr
for a handful of company; this is how she packs
her bag for days suddenly tweaked by a self-will
as necessary, comic, dangerous and predictable
as her spin-off.  The burr tangled in a bed of reeds
like a baby, restless, is not asleep,
drumbeats practicing under the skin
for summer's native wakefulness. Turning
in a nest fort and under divining hands,
I crackle like a contact mike, and know less
about the difference between panic and dream

than I do about you, the calm beside me,
living traction who keeps me still.
But then the house is a depot of strong needs.
They jostle, generating heats. Can I perform
a space for you to become the man
you are relieved by in your sleep, opening
the jewelled cabinet of your thought, without ritual
or strain with nothing but our sliding
as smooth as our—it burns my face
to think it—uncovered thrill?

Our commonness, that is, condenses
into one thick dream: we are the features
of a single future, our flesh a mixture
typical of the wrongs and rights we have afforded.
I see us rumbling along together, closely packed,
silver-tongued, syncopated. How we trail
the delivery of the stars. How we shed
wakefulness as the equipment of our individuality,
slipping into dream as our common habit.

Six weeks. Crying peak, summit of the miseries of accommo-
dation: a brain bare of myelin struggles to cope with traffic,
actualities barrelling down on all senses. Your cries now vari-
ous, expressions over the whole vocal range inaudible to us.
Abandon and comic harmonic vibrations at the end of arcs of
arousal, when you are provoked by a car seat. Large-mouthed
grunts of protest as you slam onto the uncooperative breast.
Wave forms, primitive syntax. High-pitched warnings, space-
testing yodels, coughs of annoyance, the low 'ugh' of expecta-
tion, you imitating yourself with faked cries: 'Who, capable of
no articulate sound, / Mars all things with his imitative lisp'.
You make my language a ritual and memory. I signify these
noises to keep them when you've bloomed into a speaking self
but already I'm forgetting your exactness. There you imitate
our sliding speech. Desire to join in the comedy of human lan-
guage animates you, to vibrate with such an open heart. Lan-
guage, our purpose for you and your end.

*17 August 2008, Castellina*

**3**

You can say so many things by improvising on the roots. Ma is moon, you begin to incant when dark blots the sky; it is also man, and so all people, including Dada, and which is the subcategory of the other? Or are all men Dada? And Dada, the one who would find the moon for you, is outside, where the moon is: both at work. So your pointing, your syllable is actually a sentence, transferrable impact and logic. Ma is mouth, too, is cow's bellow, is milk, now from a cup, came from Mama, now from a cow. And bu, for bunny: a request to sing. You do the gestures, wake animals who bound manically, stamping bodies in a surprising rite of spring.

*12 October 2009*

On the brim of talking your games become complex. You make patterns: here on this page, a small spider; on that page, a big one; and in the black disc of the eye, a spider: window reflection as drafter's trope for life? Butterflies flew through the humidity of the Academy of Natural Sciences in Philadelphia, their wings hairy with breath; days later, when I say 'butterfly' your palm pushes up. You follow the airplane there, remembering the trip, mellowed by exhaustion as we watched the gate gourmet load up, quaint trucks come and go. Your line of sight is modular. You're first to catch the ant's worried movements over pebbledash, and gesture with your spells to the sky, put your hand on your cheek and risk toppling to follow a flight path. You show me where the seagull is, casing the hot summer blankness.

According to Herodotus, when King Psammetichus wanted to know which was the older race, the Phrygians or Egyptians, he chose to isolate two newborn infants. Their first words were reportedly *beccos*, the Phrygian word for bread: thus Phrygian was the older, natural language of mankind. As if language as the proof of the soul, smuggled in from the other side of materiality, might also begin not with mimesis but magic—and maturation is nothing but an excavation of buried forms.

Buh-dah, your first word in the morning as they congregate for an outing to the dump. Pas-a. Pay-pa. Your imitations are bound in with your attempts to teach us your own language, whose tones and consonants we forget if we manage to echo you even once. Patiently you repeat, watching and waiting for us to understand.

*Saturday, 8 August 2009*

Few days into your seventh week and you are learning to speak. You laugh commentary to the rafters, bubble recognition of a mirror's surface shifting in immediate response to your tremors. You stare at a dry, stone wall, wooden rafters perpendicular to ceramic roof tiles, and speak tentatively to the air. While we rush blindly past local masterpieces you study these surfaces, played by bloody sunset and hilltop wind, with total concentration. Merleau-Ponty speculated on Cézanne: 'The world is a mass without gaps, a system of colours across which the receding perspective, the outlines, angles, and curves are inscribed like lines of force; the spatial structure vibrates as it is formed.' The painter prompts not a new insight but a memory; and the infant, who knows nothing of her separability from the body of the mother, is also inseparable from the landscape she shakes and wiggles.

Does what you see have any meaning? Is everything that you see for the first time brushed with equivalent wonder or indifference? Do you ever discriminate? Do you symbolize, or is it the dumb pure light that interests you in the continuous and active present? What is lost when you begin to recognize?

*22 August 2008, Castellina*

## IN LEAGUE

The glorious athlete stands out
in the field of water. Doting on the unity
of body and flattened world,
world without aperture, smooth the surface
of effort and degree. This category
is a category of attainment; sun shines in her eyes
reflect roof tiles, and a nation.
Well cold is the water as analogue, to dive in
is to be alone in ripe skin, surrounded
by brambles speak nothing to the flattened sky.
Put her awake in her cot, let her learn
to sleep on schedule and as antidote
to the loneliness of dimpled crosses. But the
pindaric, the sole self on the brush,
career driver and company man,
have forgotten their nine months:
bodies fished out of each other in strain elation.
First I want you to learn to trust us, to be
fearless in the sudden dark. For you will be hoisted
in the arc of a cry, swung this
is our promise of mutuality
no losing no contest to claim the fold the flattened
premise of the world as your very own.


Sometimes you might give orations, your hands raised out-
ward from your shoulders and your fingers curled in Roman
gestures of rhetorical ambition. You shout, practising modu-
lation and amplitude, and look at us as if we're understanding.
Your intonation is Poundian, so is the sternness of your brow.
I recognize this position.

*2 April 2009*


Another day, another outing with you, of you, in Dalston:
dizzyingly I now have to inscribe my performance of this text

into it. I perform you, mixing simony and grace. Everything is a secret from you, and nothing is, the quick wank under the covers while you babble to the blinds. You don't care.

You've learnt a few imperial gestures. Yesterday I asked you to point out the pig, known only by its pink consistency, which hides differently on every page, and you finally got it, though you confuse the moon with the snail. Where's the garden? You point to a pot of flowers on the table. Metonymy. Who's to say you're wrong?

*Sunday, 17 May 2009*

Although you still back away bashfully from other soundings, you are beginning to jam words together. High—chair. Apple —juice. Tractor—bup [book]. Objects acquire their identity not from a singular and essential reference but in combination; descriptors help you narrow down your choices, select the particular from the general and bring it towards you. You can use prepositions to signal placement: out, in, on; but you are still verb-free, most aware of the objects as a static population of your field of desires rather than the abstract and coercive properties of action and movement.

*29 April 2010*

I have mapped the words to show how *t* migrated from *d*; *a* taught *u*. An umbrella of duck, tad, dad, dog, cat. In a shabby farm cottage on the banks of the Wye, we tested your vocabulary, asking you to locate familiar objects from a pile of consumables in front of you: baby tad, ball, lamb, duck. You begin with nouns, because the world that will persist after you is an outcrop of rocky objects and not of forces that die off in their stillness. You get object permanence along with commiseration. Still, peekaboo, clapping and lip smacking are the only forms of communication you can depend on us to reciprocate, so you ply them obsessively. In this context coming and going, here and there, are not masteries of mourning so much as invitations to perform that coerce the other players to stay, watch and help. Time, mapped and spatialized, rationalized in the interval of the game, exists only in tiny units.

*20 April 2009*


Say *r*. Not *l* not *lr* which you don't recognize
as part of your family now, say *mmmm*.
How can you, with your tongue tie,
the unknown a total grammar? Say
how you work to please, to bat frustration
aside you've learnt with that
the useless lesson
that attempts are far off from delivery,
and desire counts for nothing more than noise.


Still your only word is 'da': yes. Father. That. There. It means everything and nothing, you say in combination and sequence da ada da addda. Sometimes you whisper like a monk in a scriptorium, the intermediate stage of your literacy. 'Da' takes the place of your emphatic arm, in a rigid and straight and metronomic semaphore routine. I wiggle my fingers, you lean over and put your arms up; even this small reciprocal gesture was once beyond you. But to get to this point of signification, you have had to lose something: an Adamic capacity to distinguish between all possible human sounds. They call it 'pruning', tending to the synaptic tree. It's a reminder that universalism is not a specialism for the adult mind drunk on its own irreducibility but a lost paradise with no uses.

*28 January 2009*


Again the multitudes of you, of actions and of soundings, passes between here—library, you away—and there, the insomniac May we somehow fumbled through. I failed to notice which day your two bottom teeth, visible beneath a film of pink latex, jutted into the reality of your mouth. That happened. So has a copia of words. A week or more ago, you began to say 'mmm', and 'mamamama'. As you rolled away, screaming like a lady trapped in a burning disaster movie, you held your hands splayed and your rictus face crying 'mmmmm', 'nnnnananana', as if to say, no. But your proficiencies will not be the antidote to your destiny. Say whatever you want.

*15 June 2009*

Any book will do, from strokeable farm animals to the binary pig to the mechanical shapes of tooting boat and chugging tractor. They excite you more than milk. I put them aside, across the room, and you struggle upright, pointing and repeating with growing plaintiveness: 'dare!' The child as unappeasable virtuoso of desire, for whom the parents build a containing space, because 'desire without something that resists it is insufficient, wishy-washy, literally immaterial; it meets with nothing—nothing but itself—if it is too exactly met (as in omnipotent fantasy). But a world that too much resists my desire is uninhabitable, unliveable in', Adam Phillips contends. So our few no's must keep expanding, without trapping your personality in them; we give you capaciousness with our affirmations, taking you where you want to go, handing the litany of items you point to along the conveyor belt that leads directly to the floor, in order that you won't feel closeted with 'no', barricaded and besieged by it. Feed your fantasy of omnipotence and feed you into the modern crisis of unbridled narcissism, dress you in our servitude given like a godmother's last-minute defection from the curse of your teenage death.

We serve you this way even when you're clearly intoxicated with choosing. Dare, dare, dare: the object is brought and batted away, the desire shifts with the sign because the desire is *to* sign, to force reciprocation. 'Dare' displaces names which used to be your unique reality: too consumed by the relative pronoun, the 'that', to waste time naming and being named.

Though when I ask you where the tree is, you know to look up at the sky.

15 June 2009

Your own name. Before today your name was 'Ada' (ardour), prodigy of the first bubbling over. The film of you singing in joy to the mirror is tracked with 'adā', the stress on the second syllable. Your name was an exhalation of joy, automatic in the mouth when the ravishing object was encountered. Now, gradually, and with an audible concentration, AYLA slides out. So 'No! Ayla' can become your motto, accompanied by an imperial finger curled to the centre of the breastplate. You will not devolve, even when it means much more work for you. You will shimmy down the stairs without help, peel off the tractor sticker and feed yourself. Naming yourself, you target and make your operations explicit but you have surrendered your identification with the world as a totality: you will never again have that spontaneous ability to reflect the immediacy of things through sound. Naming yourself, you give up the originality of your consonance with all your ecstasies— from now on you are one of many, 'cured' of your infancy and your uniqueness, a patron at the cafe of brewed-up situations. The cost of social competence and even power is the awareness that you are a replication.

9 April 2010

You are experimenting with prosody and pitch. You've discovered the upper registers, and hang about on high notes, in celebration of the way the balloon floats and is light. You are gleeful when your voice carries in a far room, and you shout on the street your 'a', your 'a da'. I remembered reading that iambic pentameter was conventional because iambs are the natural stress patterns of English, but apparently infants find it easier to discriminate two words in which the first syllable is stressed; and your metrical line is all mixed up: ā da, da, a dā. Entering the circle of your culture by learning rhyme will be a late concession, whatever the nativists say. In a pizza parlour on Friday you gorged on focaccia and sprung and unsprung to the 80s' soundtrack, bodying forth rhythms. You'd never been any place so loud in your life.

*25 March 2009*

In Cape Cod the waters bloomed into rose-hip, cherry-ripe and cowslip, yellow fern and dark- green woods, pushed gently against blocking stones where you tapped out small crabs under your webbed feet. You sailed on the 'water party', angry at impediments to the deep, hubcapped in armbands and dinosaur floaty. The sea is mercifully flat and silver, giving you a field to practice levitation. Obsessing over *The Gruffalo*, you played all roles in a short stand of trees between the vacation housing and unmade shoreline: 'Silly old owl, doesn't he know? There's no such thing as a Ayla!' Unmaking yourself as a joke. You also unlocked your capacity for metaphor. The dark-blue cereal bowl is the night bowl, your light-blue one is the day bowl, full of sea milk. The crescent moon which pops magically back into view is a heel of bread. The sun going down is eating the water, going to sleep and who will wake it up? Ayla!

*18 August 2010*

# 4

By lamplight he delights in shadows on the wall; by daylight, in yellow and scarlet. Carry him out of doors,—he is overpowered by the light and by the extent of natural objects, and is silent. Then presently begins his use of his fingers, and he studies power, the lesson of his race.

Ralph Waldo Emerson, *Domestic Life*

Sunday, Mother's day. M brought you up with your head wrapped in white ribbon, breakfast, balloons and pots of pansies—what Poles put on graves. Later we sat in the garden behind the Filipino restaurant on St Paul's Road as twin kittens scavenged for your food. You scream with happiness at inhuman movement. Ducks who drift along the linked breadsticks, lambs bounding mercilessly in the fields after their mothers, spray-painted with the ciphers of ownership and slaughter, belled cats that pop up on a stone wall: you're greedy for touching. A new passion for motion. Mostly you nest in objects. High up in your chair you cast them down. Then watch them in repose on the floor around you, pink rattly beans. Or put them behind you, drop them backward onto the rug where they make no noise and become invisible. This is your way of accessing the past.

*25 March 2009*

You can put the plastic blocks in the redoubt made of the elephant's front-and-hind legs, and struggle it back out again, then clap yourself. You can throw the Epcot-model ball. Over and over. Repetition is calming, is edifying, is cheerful and conservative. You began by a recognition that one volume, placed within another, does not become part of that other: that matter is a permanence of distinction. You learn the principle of Aristotelian form. Incorporation was easy for you to understand given your history. Extraction is more rigorous and melancholic. You put the ball in the hole of the orange plastic ring, flip it over, put it back in the ring. You do this over and over. Your work is methodical, testing out the limits, the properties.

*20 April 2009*

# THE CUSTODY OF SEAS

To hold the crab in mind, not as it bodies
but as the citizen of mysteries, we need another song.
Between the symbolism and the actual arms
who knows what intruder. To keep you off
from a scaffolding of fear we need song.
Song runs interference, blew chab-chub
knickle-knackle around the routines at play.
The areopagus twins can see from another eye,
a spring rain of cut hair, quietless head,
but there is no way to see you thinking other
than in your autocratic things.
Play is a system of warnings and not
in that arousal where you couldn't,
learning your themes. It's moralizing,
like the companies of trains. Agents
drafted for a kicking include the crab,
no friend to you on a slippery cosh, but here
happy to stand on the line. Include General
Patton and the mad-hatted Indians,
and a baby stiff as a peg. Far from animate,
they just stand up to the lesson,
whose outcome is steep repetition
the rituals that promise return or not return
but the silent acquiescence of objects.
Away! There's my cue, to make myself
as visible as a mask, while your bond to the crab
—crab who sings you down—will always be too deep
to fathom, slip between home block, in the mind.

*14 June 2010*


'As we age, the decline in the rate of object-play coincides with
decline in synaptic density in the cerebral cortex.' I want to
protect you against decline, the coincidence of work and

solidification; but also against the universalizing love of the toy store and theme park. You have an animatronic Elmo, who whispers you closer, to declare 'Elmo loves you . . .' Because you are part of the category of all children, the set in which all elements are loveable, infinitely, and therefore toys love you, and clothes love you and the costumed culture terrorists in Disneyworld would love you, if they could get their hands on you. This is a tawdry love, a commercial appeal to the parents' desire to project onto the whole of the crowded material world a sympathy with their child, their little child, finding her way through the objects. And yet it reflects something real: that you are universally loveable, the face of the disasters annual, the cushion for humanitarian action, the impulse to protect, defend, the measure of tyranny, the political hotpot—you are all these things because you and only you can be loved, you whose personality is still screened by your expressive mammalian face, you who reach for things and put them in your mouth and have everything but speech, and so no capacity for immortality.

*24 February 2009*


The picture-book world is either too mundane or too occult. I don't want to waste your time with housework in a suburban semi, the embarrassed bear doing the gardening as the health-and-safety worm shouts abuse. Spot in the kitchen: dog with his spit-fire markings, he is up to no good. These inductions into BBC morality, retreats practised by every train who ever wanted to stand out. But the books are your school for categorization and consequently irreducible. How do you collocate this painted shape, nothing but lines and indentations, with the roving machines you love so much to watch in the park? Why should you trust the bizarre categories we are establishing for you: dog, toad, house?

*11 May 2009*

The missing cityscapes in our books force us back to the farm. Purified farms, round and nostalgic and empty of death. The ubiquity of these farm books is the only residue of the ancient history which could not distinguish the child from an animal. Childhood is *'l'état le plus vil et le plus abject de la nature humaine, après celui de la mort'*—a gross abjection of the rational spirit in its coat and trousers.

For you, free from the history which stabled you, the dumb beasts offer simple correspondences: this is the shape; this is how it moves; this is the sound it makes. At the city farm you pull the goat's ear, and fear the rooster's crow that hurtles out of nowhere. The dogs in the park, even the big, bruising, bullish ones that tussle and turn nasty on their studded leads, attract you; you say 'deer', or sometimes 'doh' for dog, and pull the cat's tail. To school you in pastoral seemed stupidly anachronistic, a kind of protectionism; the barn door as barrage for the reality of trashy, violent localism. But maybe it's a kind of ontology, which is anyway your current business. What is the animal? What is the human? How does movement, coat and sound distinguish each species, interrupt the flow of information through occupied space?

So you learn to read images and recognize patterns in hugely various styles, for example, how is the bird in the Maisy book, with its thick outlining and rude graphic flatness, the same as the parrot pictured in the book of colours, and the pigeon ruffling the cherry tree out back and the computer-generated roundness with its triangle of pink beak in the stroke book? You must find my accusation of birdness incredible. But there it is, I'm telling you the truth. No, that one is a grasshopper.

*1 July 2009*

# TOTAL EMPATHY

Feeds bread to the sun. The sun atopic
with spikes for hands, is reverse-engineered
into the farm scene or flat pixellate,
recognizing it in these disguises is
a step in the right direction. The images, luke-
warm in the wardrobe: a drench in style
they carry charges, or sometimes don't.
Gather together the weak and the strong fixes,
apidexin in the powder blue
the greater light and how the lesser.
Or a dog in space, resident
of the same category as the pencil sketch.

Only filing down is a trick on symbols,
a way of catching them up; it narrows
the categories for random inputs (statins)
and tidies up the relations in the fixer parks.
Heavenly goes this gesture, Roman, ambivalent,
as the fist with the bread in it lifts the sun.
It's not that you have failed to recognize it,
big blood globe, big racist shiner. It's that empathy
as such has no knowable limits;
the early days are an encyclopaedia of tumbles,
and each dog that takes the twist,
each flipping mafioso car and bruiseless melt-down
Noddy that beats its head against the table leg,
shares your category. There are no spectres,
no spirit: but the matter is in each instance
full of you, and your capacities for irk or caution.
Following the dog at risk (side effects) of flushing.

This spectrum tuning would be too much to carry
        so you forget it slowly,
brush the bear and the mouse off your shoulders.
But the lesson sheaths the sun in plastic. Diffusion
of some forced affinities is a recriminated age,

and though the dimensions are amoral
to speak fluent categories is to disown the luck
that sometimes comes with passionate conformity
to all the things zippering their space.


One anthropological explanation of play is that it wards off
obesity would make you slow, vulnerable to predators. As you
run, you burn off fatty income and the risk of infection.

This sedimented relation of play to death means your objects
are full of pathos, like the red and blue spoon that blanches
under the scalding food. It's the correlative smallness of these
blunted colourful things, each innocuous, safe to suckle,
imposing our hopes as products on your brief life. You wear a
jacket to bed. It has cars on it, with curlicue exhausts that say
'on an adventure'. Shift the context to break the heart. '*Des
fleurs magiques bourdonnaient. Les talus la berçaient. Des bêtes
d'une elegance fabuleuse circulaient. Les nuées s'amassaient sur la
haute mer faite d'une éternité de chaudes larmes.*' How can we
preserve this openness, when anything is and is not an adven-
ture, taking you beyond the miniature interior that you know?
A first horse goes by. It snorts. Expressionless you scan the sub-
urban semis and rutted fields, it's all of a piece. And this is your
kind of keenness. A piece of newspaper will rouse it. Objects
pander to you. The world has to be remade to fit your grip.

*28 January 2009*


You have a hand. Lying on the playmat with its fish flaps and
blinking shells, stirring the air, you accidentally tapped the
dangling octopus. This serendipity turns, in the course of an
hour, into curiosity at your own effectiveness: find a way to
connect again. Toy eyes sing with smiles in the schematic,
primitive face. Your omnipotence descends from the general
to the special as you lift your arm and strike. Hurray for the
ready-to-hand. Hurray for the ontic. What could be more pro-
found than this discovery: you have a hand. Your hand can

do things to the world. Matter appreciates you. What an outing. I videotaped it and, days later, accidentally deleted it.

*Undated*

You tilt your head from side to side, testing the stability of objects against the motor of your own perception. You can pull a ladybird out of a pot, and the rainbow-coloured rings off a spindle in order: discovering that matter retains its discreteness even in combination, the stability of form and structure. Your pincer's improving, though mostly you curl your thick fist around objects in the grip that kills, trying to edge the apprehensible toward some angle where you can use it. You pinch us, searching the cavities of our heads, making ulcers, plucking teeth, surprised at how deep the mouth is.

Staring out the window calms you; you watch for the truck, the red bus, the house. Hearing a bird you stop, look up, wait like a predator. Contemplating the sky, you slouch back in the baby swing, and all my antics don't distract you from the zen puzzle of bar, chain and shouting against the flat grey over. You rip a dried apricot, grinding your gums and guzzling madly like a mastiff in a festival hall. Serving yourself, barely managing to juggle the slippery rice wedge up to your cake-hole. Better luck next time, the food is limitless.

All that juice and crumb makes your skin flare. Through the monitor I hear bird song, snuffles and the heating brink like a tell-tale heart, and your mitts, always going. When in a shop someone asks if you have chicken pox it makes me feverish with anger and proxy shame. This mutates into a justified greed for you, that you must skip the cream, the fairy cake or cheddar and chunky bread. That anything should make you suffer, make you uneasy in your literal skin; that it should get worse with anxiety, as we read your distress on the broadsheet of your face. Though, of course, you know nothing of your appearance and are concerned merely to use your face to keep us entangled.

*24 February 2009*

You are absorbed now by the praxis of care. The animals put down on a small padding, picked up again and patted. 'Emotional loading is absent from village make-believe.' It's the circuit of taking up which interests you. You hold each individual for seconds, forgetting the slow progress of sleep. You complicate your services, wrapping them in nappies, or propping them up with books. They recline to the same 'ah', the TV exhalation, which you use in a nest of cushions, or on the shoulder.

Rilke writes that for the child, 'the world is still the beautiful shell where nothing can ever get lost. Everything he has ever seen, sensed or heard, everything he has ever encountered is sacred to him. He does not compel things to settle within his reach. A host of dusky nomads pass through his holy hands as through a triumphal arch; his love lights them up for a while and then they fade away, yet pass through his love they must. For whatever had once been lit up by his love remains in it as an image and can never be lost again.' The rituals of discarding are not ways of managing death and loss but sanctifications—the object anointed by attention, monumentalized as image. This is a care for objects without compulsion: neither instruments of self-development or tools for jobs, your things are literally a progression whose sole purpose is their animation in love.

But why then is your care for things eclipsed by sudden anxiety? You fret at knocking, the buzz-bell or the DIY hammer poking through the confines of the house. This space must be a place of preservation, so tight and secure you don't need to think: that it abuts other homes, other goods and families, that the outside world persists as more than markings on the window. You cry when the saw rasps or the voices. But also you want to lift the net curtain, because the reflection of the light bulb is the moon. A powerful confusion.

*29 October 2009*

The house is lungs, experienced as ears.
What comes in goes drops to the big air.
It is keeping them alive. It is approximate,
the drills and collections are tapping
the crust testing its resolution to not sell.
To think in duplicates is a fear unconsidered
so far. Could there be another? Call it a man.
The man's business is his own, but is the noise,
and the dog enemying its rascal self in the plot?
Does this make all of us capable of another? Their patch
looks nothing like yours, overflowing with willow
and rusty to sedum. So no then. Defend yourself
in the house, that's where your fantasy alive
is boundless in familiarity. Familiar as sharp as a throat
pain. The seal barks in the cot. Night still presses
the strange gold bar of activities
round the monoliths of bought breaks.
If it were day, you would know by the gold
that heals the brims of the grass,
its dying attributes that slip away with
promise.


Constantly on the move, unhappy if you're left to sit in a pile
of objects, unless it's the monstrous surplus of the whole toy
basket tipped into your lap. You take the stairs in fantastic
leaps, find hazards, trap fingers and topple backwards through
thin air; you flip like a drying fish on the bottom of a boat.
The world introduces itself as categories of pleasure and dan-
ger. Overall you are full of anxieties: the sound of footsteps
coming down the stairs, creaking like in the last scene of *Car-
rie*, makes you rush for my shoulders. Anything that hums and
whirs: vacuums, food processors, lawnmowers, drills. Full of
fearfulness, also you approach strangers with neon toys,

sit down among them, give and take without malice or covetousness. So long as we're behind you, moving you along, you are oblivious, rapt in the trance of space. I guess that's our moral, discovered as you brace yourself with the girdle of your autonomy.

*15 June 2009*


You come trotting home from nursery, chub arms propelling, legs pivoting, full of bravado. But as soon as we get through the door you go all panic, want to be held up off the floor, which seems to swim with crocodiles, ants and mice and rubbish. Getting your food ready, even getting dressed becomes a struggle to unpeel you, even just the few inches that spare you a drizzle of burning fat. In the playgrounds you back away from the rush, shoulders shrugged to cold ears. I want you to grow up fearless, bold and pushy, to shove yourself through all physical and abstract obstacles into the clear spaces of your own creativity; I want you not to be skewered by shyness or anxiety, or tempered by caution. But also to realize you as you now are: skittish, ambivalent. So I must allow you to learn to cope with intermittent harm.

*29 April 2010*


Memories of the harmed child are like an origin for cinema. Freezing frames, one by one, flick past on their spindle, showing the exact shape of the face staged in fear or the ecstasy of pain, and note by note your cries sound. Imagine the enormity of real and lasting harm, how it would play in repeat and crowd out all normality. And yet, harm is a common trial: the baby boy placed by the Masai in the path of the cattle returning to the homestead in the evening, the Bolivian peasant babies eaten by the mountain spirits, infanticide of the Ache who are born without hair, death *a mingua* among the deficient infants of northeast Brazil, the Chinese drowning bucket, the Mayan children floating in the *cenotes*, the Beng snake-baby whacked with stones who feels no pain. Birth is not a beginning but the deferral of that beginning, until ritual strips away the animal or the ghostly and the child can become human, i.e. real. Was your realness to us a grand delusion? A cultural myth, the shortcut temple of our impoverished secularism?

*Saturday, 8 August 2009*

What is a month to you? A trip to the States, a menagerie, puddling, skills. Nothing but gains. Slighted repose. 'She learns to use her no for comic effect.' The power to suck through a straw.

As M settles down in the glider chair, you shake your head no: it's not time for snoozing. You can even pick out the particle which negates a sentence; if I say 'we're not going to have any milk now', you shake your head no, transforming negation into ritualized agreement. Or I tell you we're going to the playground, and you thrash and arch your back. Have you never wanted to go to the playground? Or are just relishing the talent of negativity, because the particular will expresses itself more clearly by negating the real than by asserting its alternatives? If only the good will remains good without limitation, utopia will forever be too advanced.

When we get there, the lesson of the playground is that gentleness facilitates the rules of private property. You can have it for a few minutes then you will have to give it back. The potential for collectivity replaced by toleration of temporary relinquishments, the palliative never overtaken by the redistributive. The lost ritual of the childwealth exchange leaves no ceremony for incorporation into a society based on privatization.

*Saturday, 8 August 2009*

Eater of sweet nothings and rough trades, she opens
the sky with the flat of her hand: troughing bird on the azure
speedbelt is there, cushioning cheeks. Those cheeks
surprisingly hard, unripe, as the car burred
razzles the street and soap bumped explodes
galaxies in the gutter. The button. Specimens
of natural history turned and weighed, solids
and liquids clash velocity calculated and the sounds—
bump over tiles. Constant science without stewardship.
The adventuring ants, pismire and artistic colony,
along the incline to the airplane's open track.
Reserved from the damages of reading, all the gruesome
news in the locals: machete murder in pub garden;
mum and tot in acid attack; cyclist dies in road horror.
Nature full of characters, has no premise for death
but only fullness: the cascade of venues. The playground
teaches from its cushioned ground up; but here there is
private property. No, that's not yours. Give it
back. That's hers. That's mine. The potential
for collectivity trained out of them.  All the anger
of a denied commonality is twisted into politeness,
'respect for others', the rule. So our form of coexistence
is at first premised on denial of everything we could really share:
what we see, what we know, the endless learning details.


You have begun to animate your toys. You feed blueberries to
the spongy cow, say mmmm, dramatizing everyone's roles.
Things are not just things but avatars for life, speak-easy and
hungry. You rock them, and yearn for bear and rabbit in
storms of tears. Run past dioramas of preserved animals in
the museum, excited by recognition and the surprise of scale,
trying to catch the blue tongue of the skink. Mostly though
it's machines. The wheel, the turning, grinding things practi-
cally animate that roll from nowhere down the street. Trucks,

diggers: you point out their bird claws, greasy pistons, their people keeping in small cages they roar all over the vicinity. From blocks away an ambulance's mating call undrowses you; you cock your head to locate the motorbike and the healing engine. We watch the woman next door oiling and sudsing her Mini. White froth pops into stars, run-off decorates the gutter and goes into a special nowhere. Icicles of washwater, stalactites of soap, clouds condensing in oblong pools. You point and dance round them in constant speech.

M finds a tiny leech curling blindly under a stone and you try to eat the pointed shards but it's not really all that hazardous, even when you go further into the brown current of the Wissahickon than I meant you to. Things in the sky, and things that fall to earth, how you in your admirable smallness, positioned to scrutinize the ground and crane past everyone to the sky, connect high and low, heaven and *terra nullius*.

*Saturday, 8 August 2009*


You offer your rusk, your piece of melon, role reversing, wanting the power of beneficence. However replete this generosity is, it is also social: an imitation, where you once would only take. Is this—not your infancy or my motherhood but both together, in-mixed with the writing—the 'fantasy of totality' or of 'narcissistic completeness' which Kristeva describes as a 'sort of instituted, socialized, natural psychosis'? The consequence of a fantasy of plenitude projected onto you as an 'unconscious form of self-mockery'? The ground of a particular charity? Or both: charity as psychosis, self-humiliation required to recognize another's need; floods of kindness that pour through the birth-breach in nature?

*28 March 2009*


I've said so little about you, about the infinite days, the generic things that serve your apertures and desire for fun, also always particular, glorying in the sunlight of immediacy. What I haven't written down will disappear into blanket sensation, do no justice to what you are keeping.

When you're full you have no expression for frustration. I turn you away from the beaded chainpull of the window blind, from the exuberant lightbox, and you never cry; are you happy to be ruled by us, or is the novelty of all products enough to dissuade you from attachment to the thing in hand? M says that life will become more complex for you. But surely it is complex enough already, encountering the world undiscriminated by categories, surprised by all geographies, subject to the whims of your carers, migrating with us around houses and tasks which have no meaning other than the close-ness of a hip. You face this puzzle with equanimity, watchful as a meerkat. And can't even smooth a crease out under your head, or rub your cheek dry or scratch your foot.

*9 March 2009*


No ways are open to her, unless she pivots
brain-soft in a barrel. Like a kid in a sweatshop
but with love, and every human comfort
so much from all sides: fizzing over
bracing, little canes. So she is pinned to the hip
and swings a flying chain, she waves, is all over
the shop, and presses regularly the half-smile.
She is proud, to stand, head up and head forward
buzzing outward the rude blatant
as her humans, any humans, talk.


You make relations everywhere, 'with trust in new joy'. How do you experience them? Did the old people on our outing to Aberystwyth, the boring painters with their daily residue of leaf, look like leering heads out of a Roman Polanski film? You seem genuinely democratic, shaved of any standard of beauty or niceness. And anyway they meant well, and you took them well, leaning your head to the side seductively, your courtliness a first pretence.

*13 April 2009*

Our dancing day. We sing in the rain, twist and turn and drop, kick and buck. We loft a rainbow-coloured parachute over the heads of cabbage-patch babies, lolling on pillows in a line. It flaps and comes closer, then shoots away, rippled and taut and waving. They gasp and stretch for it, their whole bodies exercised with wonder. After that there are bubbles, and you squeal and stretch warily; random movements burst on cheeks and zing through the air. This interest is of a more scientific kind.

You read people carefully, studying their intentions towards you. Will they help activate your desires? Are they hiding some malice? You poke around inside them to find out where the noise comes from. The paradigm of infantile excess, which moulds containers for extremities of feeling through the mirroring that the parent does, seems all wrong—a hyperbole of adult empathy for the paraplegic. You come already equipped with a tolerance of your own limits, and your regard for us is clement. After all, your whole life depends on our willingness to feed and warm you; maybe you feel you're earning that.

*12 March 2009*

These bags of gas and sludge
—who leak like you are sometimes
as beautiful—
are everywhere. They do complicated things
with droppers, cogs and sauces, hurt and malign
you don't, your will so far is wholly peaceful
and for that they ascribe to you
primitive rage. Ingestion

the only recognizable principle, you train
as those nubs file their way up into a soft mouth.
And each time you are lifted
you open them to stroke their teeth.
Why be afraid, be anything less
than indomitable in your gentleness?


Cast round through the days, popping up unexpectedly in
alien marshes where you have trouble echo-locating, but you
cling to the surfaces, the ledges stacked with books and the
grass candied with daisies. You are tentative, the exploratory
instinct grappling with the homing one, to step forward is to
require a catching backdrop and always you cling to the shoul-
der in doubt, looking across the side of your face at the
stranger you no longer immediately trust. Fear overpowers
curiosity, though you are still boundless and Chaplinesque,
pulling at the white tablecloth to reach the knife and the stack
of plates, weaving among the bodies and the careless cacoph-
onic residuum of a world structured as comedy.

*11 May 2009*


But not static. Unhappy in repose, you arch your back into
fish pose, press with your head to lever yourself tentatively
upright, forcing us to walk you. You toddle into the shed,
where towering boxes expose canyons and rifts. You stick
your hand into dark passageways, finger crevices. If you'd been
moving round all this time, would that also make me treat you
more like a person, the Platonic soul defined by motion, in
flight and travelling, colonizing space?

*6 May 2009*


You're walking everywhere now, even carrying appliances; no
need for your hands up palm to the ceiling to totter like a Pen-
tecostalist. It took all those months to persuade you gradually

to relinquish crutches, clothes, fingers. In the bumbling beautiful Pyrenees, we exorcised your doubtfulness every morning, cudgling you into walking between us. It was all smiles. You sometimes went for the dog, the *chat sauvage*. By the time we came back you had basically surrendered the tokens of falling, and took all plumps in your drunk stride.

*12 October 2009*

Father's Day. Your first steps. As we sat round half-looking, you turned from the climbing frame's guidewire to pitch yourself into open space, towards us. You shook your destiny, upright species, *sprezzatura*. You were proud, and we billowed round you like topless nets.

This was my due date, the longest day, anniversary of that intense and bridled period of expectation: since I began writing this love letter to you, how you've changed, the wet rustle of your growth contained in your expanding slick of skin, the field of your awareness expanding from the dumb circle of our two communicant faces to the playgym's jangle field to the room to the world. It's hard to believe that your gross of capacities is not infinite, and all acquired on the rim of a single year; but it's true, you started out limp and manic, moving sometimes like flowers sleepy in their tangled bed, sometimes like a terrorized insect, and now you are motorized and determinate, seeking out the objects of your desire, even if that object is nothing but curiosity.

*21 June 2009*

And magical, resuming. You can twist from sitting to standing, turning round, leaning over to reach the treasure chest of another vantage. You walk everywhere, and have scored yourself a large blister on your fat ankle. You favour games that involve sorting, filling and emptying. You gorge yourself on blueberries, fizz, go manic for the return of the cup. The pasta and the bells are in and out of the bowl. Most content outside, you notice the mating attack of the heavy woodpigeons in the tree, and diffusions of cow parsley and elderflower that stinks of urine. I try to teach you gentility as you stroke the Japanese maple but you are quick to behead green things, and stroke the flying ant with your foot. Chew all plastic at hazard of your life. Pitch yourself forward, and spend half the bath with your mouth open.

*3 May 2009*

Your first Christmas in America, belle of the bally, cockered for every move you might accidentally make: champion of the neonatocracy, you leave the elderly, the dying, in your noel dust. Sometimes frustrated with your inability to communicate or manoeuvre, your day was baubled with shouting, and by the end an almost perpetual glee. The babbling began. For the past week or two in earnest you go da dad adada, your canon referring to everything but also looking round for the real dad, the signified one. On your back you rock and roll, syncopating legs and shoulders to flip like a fish. A few days ago I left you in the company of various octopuses to make some pap, and when you started griping I found you'd shimmied your way into the chimney. The age of mischief has begun.

*16 January 2009*

**5**

What do you love now? You love the tomato pot with its stub of stalk (your fault). You love to break up the clods of mulch, poke the product marker deeper into the grub, drop the oval stone in and drop it out again. You love the abstract duck rattle. You love to take M's glasses off. You love fruit pots, smooth processed blueberry and plum, pomegranate with its deadly seeds. You love Tad, and the picture of the anteater and the fabric letters of your name. You love air blowing in your face. You love screaming. You love our noses (biting them). You love our bed at all times.

*6 May 2009*

This terrible cold. You come to bed and suckle, M says, like one of George Romero's flesh-eating zombies. The bitter pain of being shoved off the breast too early, when you'd like to linger, sipping blue liquor like a patient wasp. We all need to sleep. I need to teach you to share your needs, to share space and recognition that others have selves which operate according to their own biological logic.

I sit in the library cubicle, mournfully expressing into some toilet paper.

Of course the pain of childbirth. That effort to expel the giant mass of another living creature, how could it be anything else than riveting, literally, nailing the body into a fine point of all tension and feeling glutted on your crown.

*16 March 2009*

Bright day turned overcast, the roads through Tottenham were empty to reach a herd of cows with complex horns. The air was green, Epping Forest almost vacant, a circuit of long, straight paths under leafy fretwork stripped of its current. A week more than expected. When would all this resolve itself? Glorious bank of the future. All our talk narrowing to a point: to someone known only as a force, abstract, ungendered and unnamed. What would her face? Fanny Howe writes that 'In pregnancy a woman is more aware than at any other time in her life of the zone of the unknown. As long as her child is inside of her, what he or she is *not* is just as valid as what he or she *is*.' We cut back on watching, reading, learning, to concentrate only on your possibility, trying to prepare our compassion by a readiness for all that you were not. But this also made the week almost unbearable: life on hold, fettered to the single instance that seemed always to withhold itself.

*Friday, 27 June 2009*

# GRADUAL

l.  From an inked stick to the fact
                            of sickness, and a tick
as ordinary as digestion; doubt
                            and blood, then insist
the soft top of the paw, cat
                            in a billowy bag, out
of the sun: beginning to see,
                            blearily, the torch on skin,
and to be, asserting yourself
                            against the conformist's
band of placid fat. This shape
                            parked like a bank beside
the flattened navel, my own
                            history erased for the
duration, is either head or ass:
                            you choose to be there,
lawn ornament, wild dog or cat.
                            Then put to your shifts
trace curves like a big snake:
                            I don't like that, taken
like an astronaut out of her range,
                            among unfamiliar beings.
And one day crowned.
                            Your face will be the beginning
of your face. Even your sex
                            a coming-to of your indecipherability.
So when the sonic artist asks
                            what we'd like to know,
we are resolved to say, nothing.


We walked to Highbury Fields and into Angel, forward to
Chapel Market. The streets thronging with midsummer peo-
ple, a home tide against which we plodded trying to shake the
baby down. Living with a third now, a third reluctant to

emerge into our straitened life: the beginning of all possibility, and the beginning of its finitude.

We walked along the canal, taking slowly the brambles and narrow boats. Found an industrial park, derelict office storage and depots filled with wreckage of transport when we wanted a lungful of rural air. Fed up. Found a bus home by scrambling under the feeder lanes of the North Circular, heading for the Tesco shopping hub. Later J came for tea, orderly with her few months to go. I was almost jealous that this process was elapsing so quickly. Since childhood, whose calendar burnt open with unsurpassable festivals, there is a kind of precluded grief that makes up the pleasure of waiting.

The leaves of the peach tree, curled and blistered with annuality, fell onto bowls of cherries. I baked groaning cakes, stuffing a larder, old-fashioning the wait. A party decoration, a knotted balloon. Sent for a scan. Sufficient meaty placenta, deep pool remaining. Our last view of you as an anatomical example. The terrestrial crust of your skull, so round and whole and enormous it's difficult to see how you might proportion yourself for an exit.

## TRIPLE TIME

True life waving in silver marks
the intersection of all our possibilities:
before you know it you are
on them, a creator, mittened and brave.

The work of grazing, building an aspect
made of all our resemblances
multiplies the hope that you are
and always will be, vehicle in the world

to the good life contracted. It is no saint
already, its wet bed no bundled hayrack
we may not regret the piercing
we age with. But the light shining

from the epochal hole in the gate,
from the dark where
the echogenic pulse empties into bone
is an echo of all possible lights: the same

that emanated from you across
the impossibilities of ever knowing how,
to be called to happiness, to that resemblance.
Life worth crowning, bird worth feeding.


I was ready but felt this high and waiting. Still paused to the
world, half in and half awake, privy to our noisy secrets and
habits, guarding her own. *I type this one-handed, you stumbling
cross and graceful through the limit of your dream life, tucked in
the bend of my arm which has always been empty for you.* We sat
briefly in the park, then in the garden, taking photos on timer
with M peering round the full moon of my distension. The
mirror shows my apogee, a papier-mâché model of progress:
could I unhook this globe, reveal myself tidy and shaved and
stockinged underneath.

*Sunday, 22 June 2008*

You call the new baby Richard Rabbit, and believe that his microcosm duplicates everything we have. When we throw sticks into the agrarian run-off behind a summer house infested with flies, you allow some for Richard. You see his as a tiny play space, a climbing frame, canteen. Pre-history of our variety, the womb is a replicator, as it does that with the bone frame and concocting guts: maybe even carrying another tiny womb, like a hot nut in a thermos, *mise en abyme*. Is this a symptom of your preoccupation with miniatures—the Play-mobil kitchen, stocked down to the drain—or is heaven just such a dimension, repetition floating above our heads, consoling us at the limits of ourselves as containers?

*3 January 2011*

## FLUSH

Interned this double life, struggling without
duplication of the type that made it:
articulate, heavenly
a bird in a shell of mastic, which flexes
to absorb the struggle without breaking.

This is our device.
An emblem working by constraints
to realize the day as fully possible;
force intellectual and capable, unabridged
but bound into feeling as total indemnity.

This is our life on top,
everything is making there will be
no more dying as the day breaks
air closes the channelled heart:
restricts on exposure to a single habitat.
As our desire does, goes everywhere,
emboldening the most feeble,
pacifying the rip, flowing where
want widens the mouth.

You, the achievement split
into body and soul of hidden meanings:
Without you
nothing is possible, nothing is made.
With you are the choirs of wishes
singing in transition a strength of arias.


We'll need rations, a film. The red duffel bag is already
crammed with accessories, ludicrous now, in the full knowledge
of the crash and hammer. We are so over-ready we no longer
belong to the community of people. Around us, the ordinary
is choreographed just to keep us in a strange sun spotlight: they
are out doing the shopping. Today we turn into something else
entirely, pass through a charge and a thunderclap.

We get to the hospital early, it's hot, I'm wearing the single black cotton dress that still fits me. A short wait in the familiar triage unit, where you were turned under the curious eyes of the students, the registrar timidly failing to grip you, the consultant stepping up to pedal you by your neck and bottom into an underwater somersault. Bizarre that you should already be manipulable. We were cross at first, then reconciled with you, your tameness a recrimination of our stress.

Someone mines, busily about it. Is there
raking the cutlet as it is carried past
an orange filter. This business
belongs to you, the cramped vertex of your will
insists on it. You flip when leant on
to renegotiate your position, clip with a red hand
this infinite saturate. If the year were
a gestation, time bent on you, and the solstice
your light show as you descend
in clary sage and iron water,
how the laws would crumble
into a tomb of autonomies. Nowhere
and everywhere, occasionally brutish
as you blink for help and tremble at the base level,
you'll sleep your way down into trouble.
Here where texture and brightness wait
to shock you, where you will startle like a dreamer
at each intrusion of sense: nothing
and everything to operate, to speak of.


We're checked into our own room, full of gadgets and enor-
mous pedal bins for medical waste. The midwife straps on
two paddles, one with pink and another with blue elastic, and
we spend a long hour listening to the perilous rhythm of your
fast heart. I'm so glad I didn't have access to this every day.
The dips and swerves of it would send me loopy. Like you're
pretending to crash the car. But you're fine, strong and ready
for the impelled ending of this fallow year. In some ways it's
the most consequential of all your years, the one that ensured
you had every digit, that your heart split into its necessary
chambers, that you match side to side, that your lungs and
brain and all your mechanical and exquisitely animal capaci-
ties were up to scratch. Strange that the miracle of perfection
should be so common.

She measures me and inserts a double pack of gel. Then we sit and read the papers and giggle nervously at the noises. Animal shrieks of labouring women, sexual and private, the labour ward like a hotel corridor with ecstatic striving behind partition walls. We're amazed, looking twice at this mountainous belly, last days of alien home.

*Sunday, 6 July 2008*

We met you a year ago today, your hair jerry-curled with blood, your small purple limbs puffed and slackened with air for blood and your voice thin and upper. The birth has already sunk into fretwork and snapshots: eating pasta, watching the tennis; Rafa falls to the ground in exhausted victory and Roger is mournful. Pulling off into the dark and altruistically empty streets. The waddle through A&E, climbing the stairs alongside another woman equally slippery with pain. Vanishing into another place, through the tight echo and the cataract vision. My mind splits off. Get me out. Torso in scarlet agony. The sequence is fuzzy. In distress, the resuscitation equipment in place. I twist in the bed, trying to read the printout. Frozen with fear for you, caught in the headlights of the oncoming armoured vehicle. Meat on the table while they try to hook the sensor into your head. Now 'baby's coming.' What? Where is the process, the slow ascent I graphed and booked? The amniotic hook sharp and daring: I suspect you might be human, etc. Hot water rushes over the table. The high-pitched howl becomes a grinding, growling exertion. She's pushing, someone laughs. The room fills. A machine is wheeled in. A man takes position. M leaning over me. He doesn't say much, his face rigid as my reflection. The midwife gives me the water jug to sip, pours it mostly down my front. I have somehow got into a pink hospital gown. My left arm stretches into the air, fist clenched in salute. Nothing to hold onto, to brace against here, other than the noises I fetch from my distant throat. The consultant urges me to push, 'we've got to get this baby out quickly'. No time to weep for myself.

My left leg pinned up. Where are you? I have carried you these long months, knowing you intimately, feeling you, and now you're stuck somewhere in between, in a bone enclosure with no reception. I can't reach you. Then the midwife puts my hand down between my legs, and I feel a soft and slick substance, the tangle of hair. It is unmistakeably not part of me, though still within me. I'm no bud blooming but an animal in the act of excrescence. My mental resources are unused, converted to body as a rigorous tube of pain and fear: and the fear conquers the pain, and the fear is love which forces you into the air to save you by force from death. Push. The pain is moving; the body is columnar; the consultant grasps a head. Slipperiness. Turning with his fingers. The body. Out. You are out. You flop onto my belly, so long. Uncurling for the first time. I whimper. Suddenly everything is defined. 2.03 a.m.

Later, the midwife puts me in a wheelchair and pedals us out into a yellow corridor, day's space for the commerce of the ill and frightened, now serene and ecclesiastical with midnight emptiness. Everything here is orderly; the paint depicts a straightened line, the field so wide and designated, your hat is much too big. I am being wheeled along into a difference: to myself, to M, to parents, to politics, to art and language, to the body, to space, and to another, a human creature, made, internal, bursting forth, containing her energies, keeping her quietness, promising everything including the revelation of who she will be, that narrowing outcome of who she is now, all ready, all doing, all in repose, the quantities within her, the fairest attributes selected and chanced, mysterious icon of all human, fusspot, drowsing perpetual sweet, sweet lovely.

*7 July 2009*

## THE DANCING BEAR

Crushed in the glove of Cirilio Diaz
flipped in an arid ocean on promised beefs:
no gold threaded pathway to contract paradise,
just mortality, people go straight and normal
survey the highlands, excavate the animal
twisting on the hip table. The actuators surround you
with clamps and electrodes, the metal sheers
busily go the mouths lollop of information. I go about
lonely work, curtained and eclipsed,
I am no other human being on this earth.
        Its story backwards, the stream cut about
to signify something in the dark shredding and dripping
and running off: where all was
just mechanical, pain an excuse for the dissolving
of language and thought into syndicated episodes, 1, 2, 1R.

Each wave of which takes up whatever ends of your
autonomy her incarnation
her quick slip through the dark
her reptilian and her human gestures
had not already frizzed and crackled:
and smashes them to bits. What was it
is pinched in bellows, straining from the globe,
about to know at a stretch and to receive the senses
like the million flaming vectors of St Sebastian,
I can't believe it doesn't also hurt with panic
feeling the funnel bone which buttresses slim pads
of detaching flesh.

        Alone with force
the whole body, everything you knew you were
a shod and possible operator—your hand gropes down,
your eyes tortured into their sockets, can only feel
hard and slick the knot of hair. Is she suffering?
Or placid squeezed to death? Up here
breathing is an equivocation,

refuses the command to live and like a chained
animal like an animal in the tooth of a trap
try to squeeze the body off and fly into
just mind but
I do anything for her, even this much: the whole
strength of my long life works for her.

                        Then she is.
                        She is silent, shocked by electric light.
Slides into view too long and wet to hold,
too perfect to angle. Light falls on the secure
garage, the delivery suite is empty. Does anyone sleep?
What dawn is it? All feeling, abstract and practiced,
breezes gentle the face she has chosen to show,
the word relentless, the work of anything
immediately thundercracks
with her first breath her heart closes
we are breathing like a fountain,
                  deep, warm, curious, ligatures
                  in secret we share the air
                  threading us to us through the eyelet
                  that forms a hard angle
                  from the new chest of her,
                  how she gives herself to her angler.

**6**

So beautiful you were today: full of laughter, speaking to us in the one tongue. The sun has gone down on my last day of leave, and I spent too long settling you in the bed from which you will be lifted by someone else. Of course, in the bad day—when you howl and arch your back in rage against all kinds of care, when I spend an hour bent over the cot trying to edge an arm free without you seizing up from possum sleep, when I catch myself smiling at the achievement of having unloaded the dishwasher—on that bad day, I desperately wanted anyone to spin you off into variety and professional patience. But now you are fixed, laughing all day and calling, now the flowers begin to push out of the ground and the air resprings and the movement comes back to our fingers: and this is when I give you over? Another person to occupy my house, pick you up when you are shining? As I sit in a meeting, biding my time, all the tedium of wage labour will congeal in a single sentence: I do this to earn the money to pay another person to keep company with my girl.

I come over all departure-lounge. Am as dry as a transatlantic aeroplane. Though I wake up most days without benefit of daylight, feeling like my eyes are sealed with grit, I am happy because you have been curled against me for hours, sucking absently, the first to be informed of day, tap us, call us, rubbing my chin with a wet glove. Your eyes crease and evangelize. You are always already awake when I open my own face to serve you, to see you.

*1 March 2009*

## SEASONS IN REVERSE

Come with me
speaking paddle to the calabash,
a fulsomeness that pops up
in a lively way
from a sexual stamp.

Be in me. The panic
run into purple velvet in the autoclave
flecks out as currency,
as medicinal droplets. It has
no levitation, now we've invested
in Homepure.

Wash me to a strangling.
I am caught mouthing
impossible at the pyrex
as it is lifted, immaculate, from the
unaided machine. Nowhere!
It is a rite, wherein my credulity
is tested.

The house full of pulses
intrusive thoughts. The message
in the bottle which the woman
has been researching for her book is a
quotation from Kevin Costner.
Would that it had not
had that meaning.

But who goes where the trouble is?
Not me. I am saving my energies
to get well. I am saving my yeah
from the Bible
by crinkling it with an *h*,
standing it in for my parents.

This is in practice a minatory
past tied up in politeness. Setting out

and hoisted up to love,
I show the burn-mark
on IMAX. Confess for a sweet

randomly generates faults.
Who could you know? What
could you do in the heat
of the hen run? Certainly
not that. Buckling the clips
into an asterisk
thoughts run wild:
a smashing occupant,
the step-child
cut out of the frame.

I will not tell now
my design, a motto
that scratches the parquet
with fabled feet: but you had
better know it.
Doubt will never prove
the best of forgiveness.
Big red
is the ultimate confirmation.


Today I spent hours standing in different places. Sometimes,
a mirror, or a window. Sometimes a light switch. I checked
the clock. I felt abused by the vacancy of your needs.

We took you to the galleries on Vyner Street. An Estonian
artist had a slideshow with text describing the extermination
of his family: not enough time to be dean and do art, so he
leaves them to the table with straps, the Procrustean bed. I
am too tired to be ironic, and outside the hard edges of hail.
At home you fling yourself backward, crack your dome on the
floor and wail at the injustices. I spend all day, every day pre-
venting you from doing this, or picking up the octopus, or
feeding you red pepper and chicken grind. We live entirely

in the present, marking the day out with its simple cycles, moving from one room to another just to kill time; the idleness, the emptiness of infancy, so much accompanied waiting for biology to catch up with the intrigue of the world. I slide through time, look round the waiting room, there aren't even any magazines here.

But time is also apparent in the lightest contour of your face, where I see the trace of the baby you used to be, now distorted, the bumble you are now all you could ever be; and the future, the stories you can tell and read, the imagination you guard, the person you will be, my expectation and a future pleasure for my life, is also there. But also we will escape from you, regain ground on our intimacies with people and objects and even our own pasts. This will be meaningless to you, you will always be the centre of your own life, always young, always most important, until, if, you do the whole thing again.

This is the boring voice of the displaced centre of the universe. You are my continuance and my termination.

But for now, there is only now, the great vehicle of your face.

*2 February 2009*

I plunge into the pool to sweeten, after the tentative restoration of sex; the three of the family becomes the tougher, more alert love of two, and then even those two bodies drop away. In the cold water I'm a single organism. And yet keep thinking: I have had a child. The green hills are across, my child sleeps on a bed. In this stretched belly, still bifurcated with a thin brown line as life, a person became intact.

Who now begins to attach specially to me. The division of labour: I am feeder, chief soother, carrier of weights. A sling of muscle lateral across my back says so. This grappling is so constant, body against body (and with body: and for), that I almost forget I'm a person, forget walking out of a building, choosing a direction, parting the air. Forget my speed. Even my prose slackens, bellies out with simple statements of fact: you are there. You look. Your angry eyes look through the dark haze of sleep into a shuttered room, heavy lid, red lid, then disappear again into the privacy of yourself. Before you were born my life was exposed to you, all the secrets of my mundanity: you sipped my drink, listened to my gossip, paced yourself to my commute and were poised in the middle of my pleasure, a bothering float. Embroiled in me, you chose occasionally to disclose yourself in the nudges. You remain mysterious, though you begin to work on us. By choosing to reveal yourself in speech and expression you bind us to you, make us work for your survival.

*19 August 2008, Castellina*

## LIKE GLASS

Behind rock light the calm of houses.
Under rafters, walk, rewalking. Married work
to skiff the striving, disorganized kicker,
to harmless stillness. Plotting the interior by
swaying we treat the learnless needs
to earn for ourselves a little hour.
The hour cools, houses return in her dark
fish eye we walk, resuming the dropped
stitches of spaces unoccupied before we knew her.

But in that hour another body swims up:
by and on surfaces more complex and more
difficult than expected in the sloping
half-rhyme of first love. Her we
feed, comfort, walking the four stations
of food, pleasure, dryness, rest to take
and move on from us into thankless privacy.
You must be moved with this different love,
relearnt by impression of our triplicate self.


Where does the erotic leave off. You stretched out, your big
back, a mobile and cranky giant more initiated into girlhood
than stretching infancy past sustaining. Your playful wrestling,
and lying draped over me in the bath, too exhausted to face
the towel and the come-down. Of course I am sometimes
bored of you and your expansive physicality—you are small,
but for all that can't be cradle-boarded against your will; your
straight leg is marvellously tense and revolutionary. But you
are also the tonic of my thoughts. Even in bed, a part of me
flies past the indulgence of my own to think of and for you,
to build the space round you—the heavy air of the shut
room—in hope and comfort. It is part of the erotic, which
may never again be free of you; and when you know about it,
my body in the unthinkable process of decay, you'll only feel

queasy. But it's this which knits the person to the world which will outlast it. Generation in double patterning.

*21 January 2010*

If the writing only apes the magnificent idea of abundance, which has now been discovered in the aura of a real girl, then I guess I should expect writing to cede to her at least temporarily. Or to dry up, rigidifying with its own supplementarity, as stills from a *memento mori* analogize the separation of mother and child, art and life, death and life.

In *Death's Duell*, John Donne observes that 'as prisoners discharged of actions may lie for fees, so when the womb hath discharged us, yet we are bound to it by cords of *hestae*, by such a string as that we cannot go thence, nor stay there; we celebrate our own funerals with cries even at our birth [. . .] and we come into a world that lasts many ages, but we last not.' Birth as a continual death, emerging out of the prison of the womb into the prison of the world. Detachment from the earth and its cruel temptations a wisdom gradually accrued. The first lesson in detachment was taught at the end of the umbilicus, unhooked.

Parturition as gradual unfurling. It isn't just the child discovering the mother's separateness, but the mother also discovering the child's separateness, and with it, parts of her own body. Kristeva describes a mother as 'a continuous separation, a division of the very flesh. And consequently a division of language'. I occupy the language which she will need; and the charter of that occupation is outlined in these cables I am writing, for and on her.

I know that she is not me, and that most of what she feels and thinks is inscrutable. But her ultrareliance makes us into a strange tandem creature. The baby is an excrescence, the mother hogtied by feedback loops of care, the giving, the taking. And the writing becomes part of this physical and mental practice of *raising*: of supporting one who gradually learns to lift herself from the sprawling crabwise chaos of her birth state, to hold her head, to walk. Pair bore forked animal.

*30 March 2009*

You start to know us and not others. From the moment of your birth you have needed to be seen, by us; your coherence as a body depended on the regard of love. When you wake I bring you to bed, strip you and press you, and we keep each other warm. We are still so much the same person that you scratch my thigh in the bath.

*16 January 2009*

Cycling home from work, pelting past the families in parks, the women walking babies windward along the canal. The context of paid work converts my memory, physical and distinct, of doing just this, into past history. You're waiting in the arms of today's *kourotrophos*, half-eyed in matching grey t-shirts, a bit of cash in an envelope. It is disorienting to be singular, eyewitness to others actively or drearily or absentmindedly going about the business of moving in the company of their children, when you're somewhere else, static to imagination.

*5 May 2009*

We're in full heat of separation anxiety just now, you grate and call when I step out of the room, rattling the bars of the doorcage. Your anxiety produces the conventional tragedy, every day, as we leave you for work. Settling you in at nursery, I watched the twenty faces of the under-twos, sat quietly and patiently round the long tables waiting for their dinner; when they ate it, no one spoke to them; and then they began one by one to fall into their bowls of food, exhausted before the slot for sleeping. And were taken efficiently to bed. In the play space, they wandered towards me like miniature zombies, drawn to the light of a still-functioning mother. Is this good for you? Will you learn sociability and independence here? Or to cope with a lifetime of institutions?

I want for you to roam. Yes, to look and be friends, but also to know the features of animals, 'to cut across the reflex of a star', to breathe and not get spotty and asthmatic in the disastrous city air. Maybe we should throw everything over, buy a dilapidated relic outside. All at sea, casting off our utopian commitments, desperate for a green square.

You are yourself, yours, and not always everywhere mine; the movement away from me that began in the anaerobic bellows of birthing is quicker, the boundary and bondery sharper and looser and the space in between filled up with what—with your happiness and mine, o'er-look'd, seen double, or our mutual distraction cast as exigency?

*12 October 2009*

## LENT CAME TO TOWN WITH LOVE
(*Harley MS 2253*)

Blooming with ants and
rounded in bird-brides goes the
porter of blisses. Black-eyed
susans flirt in the sill-pockets,
and on the high-rises the suede
notes of nights ricochet like gales.
Every creature hums
its own tune: the wrestle
cock threatens to do you,
now woe of winter has been heaved away
by the upspring from rough wood.
So their songs of fear and feeling
wilt under the hymnic heat of happiness
a convection that rings woods in gold.

As red rides the railing,
leaves cast their lemon light
to wax cold wills.
By mandate of the blown moon
by the lossless vision of the lily,
fennel and the thyme,
birds are wowed by wild blokes
miles out in the rough, on
the make. Their urging
merged with whispers like a
stream shocked to silence. Moody guys,
griping, and my sottish self among them,
are out moaning for an idle love.

By mandate of the light girl,
by decency of the sun,
brides sing into the foam.
Dew drenches the downs,
stags grunt their round needs
to beasts declared guilty.

Worms would impress under clouds
but are coupled to the private earth,
while women blush, proud with a wonder
that suits them down to the ground.
And I, for want of just one, will all this
bloom and bedding, wood foam
and froth turf, turn the city over
and live with the witless
in the flaming woods.


I am affirmed by this terrible need. Obsession reciprocated, we spin on the axis of each other's worlds. Away from you, homesickness froths in my gut, concocting all my researches into a skim of guilt. Having a child permits us to count the cost in a different currency, exposes the dull useless orientation of production towards this self-perpetuating-self, turns time into distance and the gift of presence into a big remorseless no.

Frankly, no is not a word you usually understand. No to biting, 'gentle', makes you laugh; the shaking head of the horse-mother saying stop, saying do not eat the newspaper, pick the petals, is a toy, gaming you. We cocker you, your world swollen with yes, because sometimes it feels like the only thing we can teach you is renunciation: we pay you to mimic us.

*15 June 2009*


'While Euro-American parents claim to be training their children to be independent, in fact they strip the infant of true independence', because their first priority is to train the infant to accept them as the primary mediator of their every experience. These notes are the lament of the co-dependent, relieved only by yourself, impish, shining through inscrutably, careless, and finally untrammelled by attempts to bottle your movement and sound-making within schooled and figurative thought. Does my attention give you any advantage, or do I double you up as an ego-ideal, in person to be kissed and in language to be coddled, your soul indecipherable from your body, receptacle for my drowning love?

You speak early, you see the benefit. Holding your face to my face, we have chattered since you were born. But the interaction which all these books describe as essential for your life-long good, your cognition and feeling and language and selfhood, is a local folklore; and in those societies where it's lacking, where the child is ported facing outward, or left to navigate a perilous world and learn through pain and error and the solidarity of agemates, people, of course, still learn to speak and be happy and free. 'One of the most salient contrasts between the village and contemporary, urban society is that, in the former, the entire adult world is laid out for children to observe and incorporate in their play, whereas in the latter, this is much less true.'

*9 April 2010*

# THE HOUSEHOLD OF CONTINUANCE

*A reply to Wordsworth, 'Address to my infant daughter, Dora, on being reminded that she was a month old that day, September 16'*

When you rename yourself then, catch!
you finally are grand. You choose
the most diamond-dusted
and become a civilized person. Her name
is the fastest train in the drawer.

                            To make you
upright, swallow-tailed in the town hall,
threateningly superb
and jumping off the gantry, we string the fiction
of your native rights. Turning you to face inwards
I go backward in prosody
and massacre your toys, control your exports,
and force-feed you a lesson in contract.
That's the local procedure. The family spectrometer
tunes the shading of your seductive
mammalian face, and in unicode arcs
emotions broadcast like oil over water.

I mean to make a single woman
we first require a dough-ball:
it's not you who thrives on constant attention.
The exposure of all our secrets—
prolific apes curving on a pallet—
to those who haven't got
sense, and can die in their divine animality.
Because they are not raised to account,
care there prolific,
solitude of an academic argument,
they're largely left alone to thorn,
rock wall, and bush knife, to broad play
and aunting to death, to learn by adventure.

Your feeble motions have an interpretation
which is the only thing in this world

free from stain: how viciously, and with what
incendiary magic, we fight to keep it.
To speak in surveys, the creatures of habits
that stopper feeling as can witness:
knife, the record, issues of astonishment.
For straitening became nice
through the power of books.
People will tell you that's indulgence: do sell them
as you find them.

              And love to the invert sizes,
for passive beauty, beckons from
giant individuals who've had it up to here.
Now you can name yourself, go do it.
And weed out of my papers the field notes
of a miraculous survivorship.
Come it from reading your silly face,
coupled to love which was so stupid
it tried to inoculate you against all future harm
by its intensity. Shiver the brackets of these
few controllable years. That's it.
You are in the converted factory, and now I'm
coming to get you.


You fretted all afternoon, as M and I argued over who could
help you: we're too lovesick to sit and watch the other fail. In
the night's stages you became restless, coughing and becking
like a gecko. On my chest you faltered to finally run out of
steam, slept and slept, facing me in an hourly embrace: you
have no ability to turn away into the privacy of unencumbered
sleep. You stay where I put you. You can sometimes hold up
your head, and you suck mournfully on your own arm.

There's no space in our lives you don't occupy. I've washed my
hair, am drinking red wine and listening to music, and M and
you are on the pavement. You'll be back soon and this with its
tempests and swells will have been another day of your brief
life, just three weeks old and already being coaxed towards

habit and regulation. The longer you stay, the longer you can wait, the more we can converse with each other, but that one full of mournful fixity, her gaze darkly solid and certain as it appropriates the world, where will she go? Deeper in?

*Wednesday, 30 July 2008*

There's an automatic dissonance between the memory of a place first seen and the same place when it's come to be familiar: they must be two different places. It's the same with the photographs, some so unlike who you are now, others hold your present face on a set of neat pins.

*2 April 2009*

Work. This work. Our work, yours and mine and M's. Our delight. Whose work? Is this the work? Is this notes for the work, towards the work; or about the work; or is it the work? I didn't intend when I began to be for anyone but you. But what would it mean to paper it over with 'real' work? To pretend against it? And yet, does the pleasure it gives incriminate the other work? Expose it, show up its joylessness, its venality? And them out there, the patrons of the abstruse: have they been faking it all this time? Just really craving the sentimental? I was too tired for poetry. Does that make these notes prophylactics against the real valorous difficulties, the honour of the poem?

Dawn turns into a dark morning, the air clear but melancholic and consuming brightness, the brightness of your smalls left out overnight on the line. I've reneged on sleep while you napped to try to remember all the comments I had in the endzone of half-sleep at 5 a.m. when you first woke. And now you are awake, calling, and my time is broke.

*3 May 2009*

## FIREFOX

Skin is read by the medical eye, her light
bulb the jewel in her forehead. Of its states
only one can signify perfect rest.
We think about it with boredom.
The noise of the single drill, fixing the chest
into brick in the night, arouses us
to an imagination of the rest of them,
in the ancient forest of London
all the animals, looking up quick, anxious,
ready for flight,
opening and closing and restoring windows.
Maybe we mistake ourselves, and become
more like the viruses which we live and move
and succeed and feast to host. Then
be at ease, says the machinery
rusting into daylight for the new main,
and mice curl up in the sofa bed, and in the real bed.
But ease is nowhere like quiet, and even
through the episodic night the traffic
is released home squelching and we roll
making new work for ourselves
like insects with visions.

You've had your first morning with S. You were fine, a pounc-
ing jumble all day. Laughing to beat the band. She rocked you
to sleep, the used muslin a thin memorial banner between
your dozy head and the crook of her arm. The day was short
and I retook you until now, you are playing with M, you are
listening to the guitar and going bananas over Big Chicken.
You are biting Elmo's nose. You are flipping a butterfly so that
icicles tinkle down.

It'll be fine. The words will gradually filter down to the assem-
bly point. The ease of homeliness will end too, we'll busy the
high street like other families, trying to get supplies and see

each other for what we've become the other side of a week in dispersal. I've got to teach you to get by without me or my care would stultify you. Even as I grind the food for you, I give it to you straight and raw: you've got to choke and chew or you'll never be able to speak.

Still I loft you up and tell you again, in this serious voice, I will always come back. I came back from making this cup of tea, and when the day is long and you are almost ready to forget me, I will come back. I promise a haunting: here, you have it in your hand.

*2 March 2009*

I think I am writing about you, and for you, but at best it's an epideictic to relation, at worst the extension of the narcissism of pregnancy to colonize your entire first year: when you begin to speak for yourself I'll have to stop, my annotations no longer adequate to the plurality of worlds. I don't want to compile a book of your quaint dicta, stuff to hang up on the refrigerator or the status update. By then we'll finally begin to know you on your own terms.

You are the vulnerability for which we invest ourselves in the present place. It's so easy to meet people these days, protective borders now full of loopholes of commiseration and admiration and happiness or the memory of happiness. All these babies, all the target of someone's absolute wonder, all variously inferior to any one particular.

But today is an off day. You've been moaning since breakfast. I'm sorry for the threat the body poses, the involvement of your whole system in the small favour of growing teeth. I'm also glad finally to get away from you, try to catch up on some sleep. But I toss and turn next to a set of barbells on the guest bed, full of nightmares that you're drowning, suffocating, falling.

So much of the writing for the babies anatomizes loss: lost time, lost spaces. What of the strange mutilation of time, stretched and skewed, so that in eight months—what have eight months ever amounted to?—you learn to feed yourself, sit up straight, stand wobbling at the edge of the sofa, recognize your people. And the searing jolt of collapsed time: the first year of your life sliding to its end. The blandness of the future, compared to that.

*13 March 2009*

The turn of the season is like an egg:
or isn't, though fragile, though precipitously
strong. To notice time
is a challenge not to grieve:
for something is coming of it,
something other than the terminus,
which is the water we drift in,
which is the sun which provokes us,
to life which is the forest orchestra
we heard only once and forgot totally,
which is the speech from that yellow head:
one less of each of these is a test
of our generosity. We must give it up to a past
sedimented with the others under our feet,
against which we are so rudimentary
we seem short-run and product-trialled.
If we can carry ourselves forward without
the hurt of a forced surrender, it is no heroism,
but all the wealth and property of our
household of continuance: brave like gold stuff,
like faces, we diet on promise
that the remainder is an infinite factor
of the unspeakable now.


London covered in, debilitated by, joying in snow: seven
inches or more, Siberian airs, North Sea waters. You're oblivious, stuck inside with a running cold and laughing all through
your dinner: it's surprise which evokes you, you delight at the
simple plosives that come from a resting face, eyes thrown
upward to indicate 'wait for it'. Or you cough, I say 'exCUSE
me' in highest camp, and you give your bawdy laugh: this is
conversation. But also nothing surprises you, so will you
recognise the innumerable frosted branches, the field used
like a scratch-card, as your park? Suddenly you tilt your head

back at the playground gate, look at the sky and startle and shake with wonder. Yes, there are trees there, wires of different thicknesses for the several species, silhouettes of seedpod and nib making a fishing net out of the sky: you think it's extraordinary, and say so.

*2 February 2009*